More Praise for *Adaptive Space*

"With *Adaptive Space*, Arena masterfully takes us where few authors have been able to, seamlessly integrating research with application in some of the most respected organizations today. It is a rare treat to enjoy a profound point of view on innovation that is also actionable."

—Rob Cross, network expert and author of *Driving Results Through Social Networks*

"*Adaptive Space* provides an innovative and important look at what it really takes to drive innovation and performance in today's disruptive business environment. There is a lot to learn here."

—Josh Bersin, industry analyst and founder, Bersin by Deloitte

"*Adaptive Space* provides us with a modern-day cypher that unlocks the often elusive and increasingly important world of innovation and agility. The 4D Framework is simply brilliant. Arena seamlessly mixes deep social-science research with practical solutions into an intoxicating cocktail that goes down smooth while packing an intellectual punch."

—Greg Pryor, Vice President of Leadership and Organization Effectiveness at Workday

"*Adaptive Space* is a book that sheds a bright light on the hidden social interactions that exist within every organization. Using the mantra 'Adapt or Die,' Arena crisply articulates how an organization can positively disrupt itself by enabling adaptive space and facilitating innovative interactions. With vivid examples and a straight forward approach this book is a must-read for everyone from executives to individual contributors."

—Joseph Folkman, coauthor of *The Extraordinary Leader* and *The Inspiring Leader*

"A company doesn't survive over a hundred years without being adaptive. GM is a great illustration of a company in transition yet again. Arena's book tells how it and other companies are embracing new ideas, new technologies, and new business models. Your company needs to do the same."

—Thomas H. Davenport, Distinguished Professor, Babson College; Fellow, MIT Initiative on the Digital Economy

"Innovation is a social endeavor. *Adaptive Space* outlines four different network dimensions to unleash the adaptive potential of an organization, and highlights five principles to enable agility in a rapidly changing world."

—Kenneth Freeman, Dean at Boston University Questrom School of Business

"Most people sense that we live in the most intense time of change in the history of our species—and they're right. Those same people nearly always sense that their own organizations are changing way too slowly. They're right about that too. And it's scary.

"Now Michael Arena mines the remarkable transformation at GM led by Mary Barra to show the rest of us the key mechanisms and principles that make bold change easier, faster, more reliable, and more robust. His insights about *Adaptive Space* help you move transformation from a vague hope to a practical reality. Read it. Use his concepts. Shift from being afraid of the future to getting it to show up somewhat ahead of its regularly scheduled arrival."

—Larry Keeley, innovation expert, Doblin

"*Adaptive Space* is a terrific achievement. Arena's book creates a very simple model that leaders of innovation can use. The book delivers tactics for leaders to help teams innovate, as well as guidance on creating the more subtle and important social connections that a leader must both be building and attuned to in their organizations."

—Perry Klebahn, Adjunct Professor, Mechanical Engineering,
(the d.school) Stanford University

"Michael Arena's *Adaptive Space* is an important book on a critical issue for many organizations. His firsthand knowledge of GM combined with extensive research provides relevant, accessible, and thought-provoking insights and is a must-read for anyone struggling to increase the speed and agility of their organization."

—David Gillespie, Partner, Oliver Wyman Group

"*Adaptive Space* takes agility and innovation to the next level. This is the future. Actually this is how companies should be managing now. It truly is a must-read for business leaders, from the CEO to the line leader to the HR professional, in all industries."

—Cynthia J. Brinkley, President and Chief Operating Officer, Centene Corporation

"Adaptability has never been more critical, and this book takes a practical look at what it takes to build that capability in your organization."

—Adam Grant, *New York Times* bestselling author of *Give and Take,
Originals,* and *Option B* with Sheryl Sandberg

"I have known, and coached, for years that relationships are essential to organizational success. *Adaptive Space* will help you elevate this understanding to a whole new level by masterfully articulating how specific network connections facilitate innovation and agility. This book is an essential read for anyone who's business is facing disruption."

—Keith Ferrazzi, *New York Times* #1 bestselling author of
Who's Got Your Back and *Never Eat Alone*

"*Adaptive Space* is the best book I've read about what it takes for big organizations to innovate as a way of life. Michael Arena blends rigorous research, success and failure stories, and his experience as a senior executive to show how to build companies where people uncover and weave together the best ideas, challenge conventional thinking and methods, and develop promising innovations in focused and energized teams. Even better than that, Arena shows how companies can keep releasing new and better offerings into the marketplace—rather than developing promising innovations that are crushed by dysfunctional people and internal politics."

—Robert Sutton, Stanford professor and author of bestsellers
including *Scaling Up Excellence* and *Good Boss, Bad Boss*

"Perfectly stated by Michael Arena, 'In today's rapidly changing environment, lack of agility is the kiss of death.' *Adaptive Space* gives real insight into how mammoth companies such as General Motors were able to disrupt their strategy paradigm to thrive in a rapidly changing marketplace. His insights are based on extensive research, as well as real-life, roll-up-your-sleeves work experiences. A great read for leaders looking to disrupt and innovate."

—Melissa Howell, Senior Vice President, Global Human Resources, Kellogg Company

"Over the past few years, networks have changed the way we live our lives. Arena makes a compelling argument about how they are also radically altering organizational practices. *Adaptive Space* reveals the power of networks in generating, sharing, and scaling ideas. It is a must-read."

—Alex "Sandy" Pentland, Director of Human Dynamics Laboratory
within the MIT Media Lab and author of *Social Physics*

"Reading this book is like swapping out an old, scratched, dirty pair of glasses that once saw hierarchies for an entirely new set of lenses that make both visible and actionable the radically, positively disruptive power of networks."

—Chris Ernst, PhD, Head of People and Organization Potential,
Bill & Melinda Gates Foundation

"Incisive and immediately impactful! Michael Arena's book is that rare gem, applying sharp analytical insights from state-of-the-art science to some of the most pressing managerial and organizational issues of the day. Delivered in highly lucid prose with a heavy dose of practicality, digesting this book will enhance every executive's knowledge base and toolkit."

—Glenn R. Carroll, Laurence W. Lane Professor of Organizations,
Stanford Graduate School of Business

ADAPTIVE
SPACE

How GM and Other Companies are
Positively Disrupting Themselves and
Transforming into Agile Organizations

MICHAEL J. ARENA

New York Chicago San Francisco Athens London Madrid
Mexico City Milan New Delhi Singapore Sydney Toronto

1 2 3 4 5 6 7 8 9   QFR   23 22 21 20 19 18

ISBN   978-1-260-11802-5
MHID   1-260-11802-9

e-ISBN   978-1-260-11803-2
e-MHID   1-260-11803-7

This publication is designed to provide accurate and authoritative information in regard to the subject matter covered. It is sold with the understanding that neither the author nor the publisher is engaged in rendering legal, accounting, securities trading, or other professional services. If legal advice or other expert assistance is required, the services of a competent professional person should be sought.

—From a Declaration of Principles Jointly Adopted by a Committee of the
American Bar Association and a Committee of Publishers and Associations

McGraw-Hill Education books are available at special quantity discounts to use as premiums and sales promotions or for use in corporate training programs. To contact a representative, please visit the Contact Us page at www.mhprofessional.com.

Library of Congress Cataloging-in-Publication Data

Names: Arena, Michael J., author.
Title: Adaptive space : how GM and other companies are positively disrupting themselves
    and transforming into agile organizations / Michael Arena.
Description: New York : McGraw-Hill, [2018]
Identifiers: LCCN 2018004444| ISBN 9781260118025 | ISBN 1260118029
Subjects: LCSH: Organizational change. | Strategic planning. | General Motors
    Corporation--Case studies.
Classification: LCC HD58.8 .A737 2018 | DDC 658.4/06--dc23 LC record available at
    https://lccn.loc.gov/2018004444

"Speed, agility, and responsiveness are the keys to future success."

Anita Roddick

Contents

Foreword

I wonder if this story resonates with you. The organization you work for is producing some of the best products and services it ever has, and it is doing so far more efficiently. At the same time, revenues look great and profits are solid. Yet the company can't seem to attract new customers. And when you look out on the horizon, you see an array of non-traditional competitors flocking into your space, threatening to bring to market products and services that challenge your very core. This is my story as CEO at Best Buy.

My experience at Best Buy is an example of what nearly every organization faces today. In a dramatically changing world, we are all poised for disruption. Yet, if you run one of these companies, it's not an awareness problem; you're a skilled, intelligent leader and you can see these challenges out on the horizon. However, when you try to steer the organization in response to these challenges, it's like you're trying to steer an ocean liner, while the would-be disruptors are swiftly navigating the white-waters in an agile manner.

Since retiring from Best Buy, I have served on several boards, both public and private, for profit and nonprofit. These institutions cover a wide range of fields, including medicine, food, entertainment and media, and waste management. However, they all seem to have one thing in common. They too have an array of would-be disruptors lurking out on the horizon. It seems to be a universal challenge these days.

The reason leaders feel like they are steering an ocean liner is due to their organizational structure and culture. Their very company was built for the industrial age and we are now operating in the digital world. The challenges have been well chronicled in books like *Built to Last* and *Creative Destruction*. Yet, the solutions are not so easily found.

When I was at Best Buy, I found that people deep in the organization, that is, in the stores, had more relevant and better ideas and solutions than I had as CEO. I could illustrate this with countless examples if this weren't a foreword to a book! The core reasons why they had better ideas are easy to understand. First, they were closer to the customer. They were on the edge. They had grown up using the digital tools, which I had to learn to use as an adult. They had immediate access to almost any information on their phones that I had to wait to get in the boardroom. And they had different life experiences and skill sets. So the solution would seem obvious: use their insight to run the company. The methodology to do that is not so obvious. If you can solve this puzzle, not only are you going to be working with better ideas, but the employee who is engaged in the process of reinventing the company is going to have a much more fulfilling work experience, while helping to attract new customers.

For nearly a decade, I've worked with a team of academic researchers, organizational leaders, and skilled practitioners that have empirically researched this challenge with the intention of creating practical solutions that could be used within any organization. Michael Arena, a core member of this team, along with his compatriots at General Motors, have produced a breakthrough methodology which can be used to solve this puzzle. They extend beyond chronicling the challenge and have moved into solving it. The methodology of *Adaptive Space* provides the insight and tools that can be used to bring almost any idea to life, even in long-standing enterprises that need fundamental adaptation.

You don't have to be the CEO of a company to apply these methods. As a matter of fact, you might have an advantage in terms of using these tools and principles if you're not at the top of the organization. If you want to grow your career and facilitate meaningful impact, I suggest you try this wherever you are today. See if you can positively disrupt your organization into a more agile organization, much like General Motors has.

BRAD ANDERSON
Retired CEO and Chairman of Best Buy

PART 1

Uncovering the Power of Networks

1

The Need for Adaptive Space

You've got to disrupt or be disrupted.

—John Chambers of Cisco

Organizations are under assault. If they don't adapt, they will die. We see this happening all around us. We are in a time of tremendous transformation, unlike anything we have seen in over a century. In this environment we need to do something that most of us have not been trained to do and our organizations have not been designed for: we must learn to adapt. As John Chambers, executive chairman of Cisco, says: "If you don't reinvent yourself, change your organization structure; if you don't talk about speed of innovation—you're going to get disrupted. And it'll be a brutal disruption, where the majority of companies will not exist in a meaningful way 10 to 15 years from now."[1]

The inability to adapt or to even recognize the need to do so is what brought companies like Blockbuster down. When Marc Randolph and Reed Hastings had the idea to start Netflix,

Blockbuster was the major player. Blockbuster had a lock on the market, and its leaders were satisfied with how things were working. But Randolph and Hastings were entrepreneurs. They didn't like that if you wanted to rent a movie you had to drive to Blockbuster, hope the video you wanted was available, and then rush to return it to avoid exorbitant late fees. Instead they imagined allowing customers to order a movie online, receive a DVD in the mail, and return it at their convenience, *with no late fee*. With this idea they launched Netflix in 1997.[2]

Blockbuster responded as many organizations do: it ignored Netflix. Executives continued to focus on their core business and never imagined that it could go away. Even worse, when Reed Hastings flew to Dallas in 1990 to propose a partnership between Blockbuster and Netflix, Blockbuster executives laughed him out of the room. Their CEO, John Antioco, was considered a retail genius, known for his operational acumen and long history of success. His model for Blockbuster was working brilliantly, and he and his team couldn't imagine sharing the brand they had worked so hard to build.

In the end, Netflix was the dominant player and Blockbuster was in bankruptcy.

Positively Disrupt or Be Disrupted

Netflix beat Blockbuster for one simple reason: it was agile. Contrary to Blockbuster, Netflix embraced the mantra "You've got to disrupt or be disrupted." And that meant not only staying ahead of the game, but also *changing* it.

From the beginning, Netflix executives continually read market conditions and showed the willingness to take bold moves.

The original idea of a pure rental-by-mail service allowed them to get off the ground, but as demands changed, they changed along with them. Seeing that the pure mail service was having limited success, they morphed to a more radical approach, a subscription-based model. The new approach was launched on September 23, 1999, with a free month trial, and the response was overwhelming. Less than 20 percent of the subscribers canceled after the trial period, and Netflix grew to one million subscribers by 2003. Blockbuster responded with its own online service in 2004, but it was too little, too late. Netflix continued to adapt by moving into streaming video in 2007. However, that created new challenges. As Netflix quickly discovered, the cost structures and value propositions for mail versus streaming were creating inefficiencies and a lack of focus. It needed another solution.

This came in a bold move in 2010: the announcement of a split in the video streaming and DVD-by-mail businesses. Like all bold moves, this was a risk, and the result wasn't desirable. Rather than being embraced, the split was widely criticized by customers, and higher prices made things worse, leading to widespread customer dissatisfaction. Recognizing the mistake, Netflix decided to shelve the plan and continue operating through a single website, but the company didn't give up. It quietly pursued the transition into streaming video, and by 2016 it had successfully rebranded the DVD-by-mail service into DVD. com, a Netflix company.

Shocking the entertainment industry, Netflix changed the game once again when it plunged into original content. In 2013 it released its first original television series, *House of Cards*, offering the entire season upon release to satisfy customer demand for binge viewing. Nominated for an astounding nine Emmy awards, *House of Cards* was a phenomenal success—rivaling the best that traditional television had to offer. Its victory with viewers was repeated with *Orange Is the New Black*, *Luke Cage*, *Stranger Things*, and *13 Reasons Why*. As a result, the company is no longer just a streaming service. Its expansion to millions of consumers around the world has now made it a dominant player in the entertainment industry.

The secret behind Netflix's success was its ability to be agile, positively disrupting before being disrupted by others—that is, taking an iterative approach and acting swiftly to proactively change the game. Netflix had the willingness and capability to explore, move quickly, and then adapt when needed to engage in future possibilities. In the words of Reed Hastings:

> *Most companies that are great at something—like AOL dialup or Borders bookstores—do not become great at new things people want (streaming for us) because they are afraid to hurt their initial business. Eventually these companies realize their error of not focusing enough on the new thing, and then the company fights desperately and hopelessly to recover. Companies rarely die from moving too fast, and they frequently die from moving too slowly.[3]*

The Need for Agility

In today's rapidly changing environments, lack of agility is the kiss of death. A study from Washington University shows that an estimated 40 percent of today's S&P 500 companies will no longer exist a decade from now.[4] According to *Innosight*, the average tenure on the S&P 500 will shrink to 14 years in the next decade, down from 33 years in 1965.[5] Indeed, we have seen this phenomenon bear out in the demise of behemoth companies such as Eastman Kodak, Yahoo, Motorola, and Research In Motion (BlackBerry) and the woeful diminishment of Sears.

Potential disruptors are everywhere. Knowledge workers are being displaced by advanced technology and artificial intelligence that is changing the nature of their professions. Free calling apps are challenging telecom, financial services are being put at risk with free trading platforms, and automotive companies are being pressured by ride-sharing companies like Uber and Lyft. Even technology darlings like Twitter have experienced the attack as new, fresher platforms like Snapchat and Instagram gain popularity. The extent of the devastation is currently playing out in the retail sector. Once-prominent retailers, such as Barnes & Noble, JC Penney, and Office Depot, are clinging to life while Amazon is thriving—swallowing up market share and driving unprecedented revenue growth by continually extending and shifting into new areas of business.

The key refrains are "we are operating in a radically changing world," and "we are not equipped to respond to it." We know we must do something different, but what? We see people working as hard as they can, using what they have been taught to do, and yet no longer getting the results they want. We see companies struggling to change but not able to keep up with the constant disruptions being thrown at them.

What has been missing until now is an understanding of what the winners are doing and how they are managing. How are companies like Netflix able to succeed by positively disrupting while companies like Blockbuster go down? And can Netflix's success be replicated in large, established organizations with pressing demands for short-term success from shareholders?

The answer is a resounding yes, but it takes a new way of thinking about what it means to generate results. Results are not only about current success; they are also about future success. And that requires forward thinking and a great deal of agility.

That is the focus of this book. *Adaptive Space* helps companies see how they can enhance agility in a complex world. Based on a decade of research and my personal experience as the chief talent officer at General Motors, it will reveal how companies like GM are now aggressively positioning themselves for inevitable disruptions, such as the oncoming mobility revolution, while at the same time driving daily performance by shipping trucks out the back door. It will reveal how organizations like IBM and Amazon have continually reinvented themselves through proactively responding to potential disruptions, and it will look at how companies like Pixar and W.L. Gore and Associates have enabled agility.

The insights offered in this book come from a decade-long research practice partnership in which a core research team set out to understand why some organizations succeed at adapting in a radically changing world and others do not. After hundreds of interviews and the intensive study of dozens of organizations spanning a variety of industries, the discoveries were surprising even to the research team (see Research Summary at the back of this book). The key to success in today's disruptive environment is enabling agility through a concept named Adaptive Space.

Positively Disrupting Through Adaptive Space

Adaptive Space is, quite simply, the freedom for ideas to flow into and throughout an organization. It operates as a sort of free trade zone for ideas within large complex organizations. Adaptive Space can be thought of as the relational, emotional, and sometimes physical space necessary for people to freely explore, exchange, and debate ideas. It involves opening up connections for people, ideas, information, and resources to come together and interact in ways that enhance organizational agility. Adaptive Space enables organizations to be positively disruptive so they can control their own destiny before someone else does. It facilitates the connections necessary to provide a social bridge to transport ideas from entrepreneurial pockets found throughout the organization into the more formal operational system.

Sociologist Ray Oldenburg pioneered the concept of a "third place."[6] He argued that the "first place" for individuals is their home and the "second place" is the office. The "third place" however is a café, coffee shop, church, community center, parlor, or other hangout. Oldenburg argues that third places are important for civil society, democracy, and social engagement. They provide people with a sense of connectivity and facilitate and foster broader, more creative interactions. A "third place" is crucial for expression, connection, and growth. It operates as a free trade zone. Adaptive Space functions like a "third place" within organizations. Organizations are driven by the operational system that drives formality, standardization, and business performance. They are also represented by many local groups, often acting as entrepreneurial pockets that strive for greater innovation, learning, and growth. However, not all organizations have a third element, Adaptive Space. Adaptive Space works at the intersection of the operational system and entrepreneurial pockets within an organization (Figure 1.1). It provides the connections necessary to facilitate and foster broader, more creative interactions.

Adaptive Space helps organizations gather and distribute information in ways that promote positive disruption in order to enable organizational agility—that is, to proactively disrupt themselves in anticipation of external pressures. It encourages the interplay of entrepreneurial and operational capabilities. They must be connected. One without the other causes the system to fall out of sync: too much attention on the entrepreneurial can generate ideas that cannot be converted to results; too much focus on results can lead to a loss of innovation. Adaptive Space overcomes these problems by nurturing and protecting entrepreneurial initiatives in the face of stifling operational forces. It creates conditions for entrepreneurial ideas to trigger and develop and loosens up the operational system to make it more accommodating of changes coming from entrepreneurial pockets.

We can see this in the case of Netflix and Blockbuster. Netflix clearly had Adaptive Space that allowed ideas to trigger and flow into adaptive outcomes. Its leaders were able to take entrepreneurial ideas—at first from Randolph and Hastings but later from the broader organization—and figure out ways to develop and scale them into the operational system to increase agility. In some cases this worked smoothly, such as the move into original content. In other cases there were bumps, such as when the addition of streaming led to operational inefficiencies and customer dissatisfaction. But the decision makers did not consider this a failure that forced them to return to the previous order. Instead they learned from their mistakes. They responded by fixing the operational problems and continued to use Adaptive Space to find ways to accomplish what they knew to be the most agile strategy.

Blockbuster took a very different approach. The company did not have Adaptive Space. Instead it focused on the ability of the operational system in generating short-term results. Any innovation was incremental and positioned in the context of the current operating environment. More important, its executives never considered how an entrepreneurial idea could combine with their operational expertise to generate agility. Indeed, when Hastings brought them an entrepreneurial idea, they quickly rejected it. Because they were not able to think beyond their current success or strategy, Blockbuster decision makers overlooked the flaw that ultimately brought them down: over-reliance on the late fees that constituted a large part of their revenue stream. As described by Greg Satell in *Forbes*: "The ugly truth—and the company's Achilles' heel—was that the company's profits were highly dependent on penalizing its patrons."[7] When Netflix offered an alternative, and word spread about the more convenient way to rent movies, customers flocked to its new operating model. In short, Netflix's agility disrupted Block-buster's rigidity.

Playing in the Pressures

Adaptive Space is the secret behind the success of highly agile organizations. Like Netflix, these organizations generate both future innovations and current results. They do this through Adaptive Space.

Agility is critical for survival in changing environments. Organizations that are not agile in response to their environment are poised to be disrupted. While they might continue to produce in the short run, they will not survive over time. Agility is the key to Netflix's transformation from a focus on DVD-by-mail to streaming to a provider of original content. As the environment shifted, Netflix positively disrupted itself by proactively moving. It succeeded by "playing in the pressures."

Enabling Adaptive Space and responding effectively to environmental pressures is not easy. Generally organizations, like Blockbuster, are much more prone to shutting Adaptive Space down rather than opening it up because they don't like the ambiguity naturally associated with shifting toward new possibilities. They would much rather maintain a limited amount of control over the current realities, even if it is shortsighted. Organizations and leaders that are good at enabling Adaptive Space, however, know that pressures are needed to loosen these otherwise rigid systems for change. They "play in the pressures" by leveraging the encountered difficulties to enable Adaptive Space. That is, they create connections to seek out the opportunities associated with inevitable disruptions. This is exactly what is happening at General Motors (GM) under Mary Barra. Barra, GM's CEO, knows that the pressures facing the automobile industry are disruptive. Therefore she is "playing in the pressures" to help GM "positively disrupt before being disrupted."

To do this, Barra and her team are taking bold actions to enable Adaptive Space and facilitate organizational agility. Like all automotive companies, GM is facing increasing demands and pressures from its environment, threatening the industry as we know it. These demands are arising from a combination of forces coming from the convergence of shared mobility, emerging technologies, hyperconnectivity, and new business models. The changes are expected to expand the total revenue pool of the industry significantly over the next decade, with advancement in on-demand mobility and data-driven services as the primary impetus. The disruptors are already positioning themselves, with tech giants like Google, Apple, and Intel flocking in for their share of the revenue pool. Ride-sharing businesses like Uber are transforming the automobile from a consumer product to a service platform, while electric vehicle advancements and autonomous technology are ushering in a revolution toward self-driving vehicles that will change mobility forever.

In an attempt to break the incumbent paradigm, GM has taken bold actions, activating Adaptive Space around multiple entrepreneurial pockets to get ahead of the mobility disruptors. First GM invested a half-billion dollars in Lyft, the ride-sharing rival to Uber. A month after that, GM bought a Silicon Valley start-up, Cruise Automation, to catapult forward on the autonomous vehicle frontier. The company then unveiled the Chevy Bolt, the industry's first affordable long-range electric vehicle. Following this, GM launched its own car-sharing platform, Maven, to compete in the urban mobility space and aggressively scaled it in the first 12 months of operation.[8] Each of these activities alone is critical, but it is the Adaptive Space that surrounds them that has the potential to help GM positively disrupt itself. That is, it will be the way people, ideas, information, and resources come together and interact across these pockets that will enhance organizational agility.

Although each of these activities helped position GM for success on the new entrepreneurial frontier, perhaps the company's boldest moves were completed within its operations space. Moving away from unprofitable or unpromising businesses indicates the automotive giant's willingness to shrink a company that once prided itself on being the industry's largest and has helped loosen operational systems to become more agile. GM made critical strategic decisions in the legacy business to free up the resources to invest in the high-tech future of mobility. For example, in 2015 Russia showed no sign of improving sales as an emerging automotive market, and amidst the collapse of the Russian ruble, escalating interest rates, and deepening political turmoil, General Motors did the unthinkable: although GM owned 9 percent of the country's market share, the company announced it would stop selling vehicles in the Russian market and indefinitely idle the six-year-old plant in St. Petersburg.

In 2017 the company made an even bolder move in selling off its entire European business, Opel Vauxhall, which had lost nearly $20 billion over the previous two decades.[9] This was part of GM's effort to scrutinize investments on a case-by-case basis. The goal was to identify any operations that didn't have a significant chance of being a dominant player with sustained profitability and redeploy resources into the future of mobility. This led to other decisions in international markets. For example, in 2017 GM also declared that it would exit the India market. Despite India being projected to become the world's third-largest auto market, GM was having difficulty turning a profit there. GM also announced that it would pull entirely out of South Africa, selling its manufacturing operations to Isuzu Motors. In a statement about the move, Barra said, "We are committed to deploying capital to higher-return initiatives that will enable us to lead in our core business and in the future of personal mobility."[10] Barra and GM are thus investing in a multitude of entrepreneurial activities and freeing up critical operational resources to open up Adaptive Space. The company has demonstrated the discipline necessary to become more agile by shedding unprofitable businesses to become more fluid and responsive. GM recognized that these legacy businesses would consume resources and limit agility. However, GM's ultimate success within the emerging high-tech mobility frontier will be determined at the interface of these entrepreneurial pockets and their operational system, within its Adaptive Space. Adaptive Space is where the potential to enable ongoing idea discovery, development, and diffusion across the organization can be found. In the end, triumph is not about the strategic bets placed. It is about enabling social connections for Adaptive Space.

4D Connections of Adaptive Space

Unlike traditional organizations that rely predominantly on human capital strategies for innovation and growth, Adaptive Space leans on social capital strategies. Human capital represents the talent, experiences, and competencies that are present within an organization. Social capital can be thought of as the competitive advantage that is created based on the way an individual is connected to others. It represents the relationships and interactions within an organization. Therefore, human capital is about what someone knows, while social capital is about how well someone is positioned to leverage what he or she knows. Both are essential, yet organizations have overemphasized the former at the expense of the latter. Consider an analogy from physics. You may recall that particles and waves are two properties of the same thing. For example, with light we have photons and we have the flow of photons respectively. A particle has specific mass, volume, and density, while a wave has velocity and frequency characteristics. Both particles and waves are important, but traditionally, only one could be evaluated at any given point in time. The same is true of human and social capital. Both of these are critical in organizations, but up until now we have only measured and evaluated human capital. Adaptive Space challenges us to see the complementary value of both. As with particles and waves, one provides potential and the other velocity. Human capital provides organizations with the intellectual capacity or potential to drive change, while social capital focuses on deliberately positioning this capacity so that it can be swiftly leveraged. By opening up Adaptive Space, organizations are able to tap into existing intellectual capacity, while also moving with speed. They are able to increase the velocity of idea flow into and across the firm, therefore increasing agility. Most organizations don't suffer from a deficit of ideas or human capital potential. They just need to create more deliberate connections. Organizations need to focus on the flow of these ideas by paying more attention to the waves that are being generated on the social front.

Adaptive Space works by facilitating connections to enable information flow for the discovery, development, diffusion, and disruption needed for organizations to innovate and adapt. Let's call these the 4D connections of Adaptive Space. Discovery and development connections are represented by an individual's network position as either a broker or connector, while diffusion and disruption connections represent the emotional shift in energy within a network facilitated by either energizers or challengers. Together, the 4D connections provide the velocity necessary to allow innovative ideas and operational constraints to collide and combine and form novel solutions and outcomes that respond to pressures from the environment. Adaptive Space thus acts as a conduit to more fully leverage social capital and actively transport ideas from the entrepreneurial pockets throughout the organization into the operational system by enabling 4D connections.

2. Development Connections

Adaptive Space also enables connections within local teams to facilitate idea enhancement. Individuals limited to cohesive subgroups are less likely to come up with bold ideas, but they are highly proficient at developing ideas. Isolated discovery is inadequate without further development and application. Ideas alone are cheap—to be useful they need to be socialized, developed, and applied. This is where development connections are so critical. Local entrepreneurial groups are more likely to have higher cohesion, meaning they are more likely to have individuals who are connected to one another. Therefore they provide a more appropriate context for idea elaboration and refinement.

Research shows that cohesive groups typically demonstrate higher levels of trust and are able to quickly share information across the group. This makes them ideal for the processes needed to develop, refine, and elaborate novel ideas in ways that make them more amenable to scaling. In particular, high levels of trust within cohesive groups facilitated positive affect, learning, and risk taking—all considered to be crucial components of creativity and development. Ideas socialized in cohesive subgroups are more likely to be accepted and ultimately applied because they can be shared more easily, and local application appears to enrich early learning and enable continuous enhancement through multiple iterations. In a large technology organization I researched, local teams were encouraged to build prototypes of ideas they had considered throughout the week. On Friday afternoons, the groups would then hold tryout sessions to test these new prototypes with each other. The most successful ones would be tested repeatedly during the following week. Then the enhancements were shared once again the following Friday. The

1. Discovery Connections

Adaptive Space fosters connections that trigger nov
insights, and learning that lead to adaptation. T
process is often inhibited by siloed structures that l
new insights. Deliberate interactions open up acce
novel ideas. Adaptive Space encourages individua
beyond their local subgroups and follow their inn
explore.

Brokerage is key. Brokerage facilitates the dis
through the generation of creativity and the flow
Brokerage represents the bridge connections bet
occurs as individuals act as links from one group
result is a generative conduit of fresh ideas and i
increase the probability for adaptation. In one
research team studied, this was accomplished u
"pitch days" that allowed any individual to se
slot and present a transformative idea to a
panel of leaders. If their idea was selected,
encouraged to recruit an ad hoc team of colle
perspectives to continue the discovery proces
broader concept.

Brokerage triggers the emergence of n
intersection of existing groups. As heteroge
act, new insights and discoveries emerge.
provide the thought diversity and ideologic
spark creative thinking. When everyone t
it is hard to identify alternative approache
operating. Brokerage provides discovery
people, information, resources, and tecl
and generate novelty, innovation, learnin
organization.

result was a steady flow of new products and services locally. Development connections provide a climate to get things implemented locally.

3. Diffusion Connections

Adaptive Space enables interactions to move concepts from development across the broader organization to enable broader diffusion. These connections facilitate a linking-up process in which ideas move beyond local development into the broader organization to aggregate for scaling. Local implementation provides only limited value to the broader enterprise. Cohesive subgroups that are isolated from other groups are more likely to have their ideas dismissed by the broader organization. Moreover, although cohesive groups work well at implementing incremental changes, they are far more limited in promoting bold change. This is because individuals within a cohesive group are less likely to trade off their status within the network for risky ideas. Fortunately, Adaptive Space enables diffusion connections to advance ideas beyond local networks so they can flow easily into the broader organization.

Adaptive Space helps drive diffusion by engaging network energy. People in the network who are energizers amplify ideas across the organization because they are also motivators. They have a unique ability to attract others to an initiative and convince them to take action—people seek out energizers for information. The energy generated then motivates others to engage in interactions and devote more discretionary time or resources to an initiative. Energizers, often in partnership with brokers, thus enable new possibilities by integrating different expertise or backgrounds.

Furthermore, high-energy networks create positive connections that enable ideas and concepts to spread quickly. We saw evidence of this in a large medical devices company we studied. The company had assembled a powerhouse of superstars into a centralized innovation team to disrupt itself from within. A team of nearly 30 high-skilled individuals gathered daily to build new concepts and business models. They even engaged the device users through design thinking and prototype testing. The result after three years of existence was zero commercial products. Management had no choice but to disband the team and redeploy the resources throughout the broader organization. Then something remarkable happened. The very same concepts that had been created by the central team started to gain internal traction. It turns out these individuals didn't lose their conviction about reinventing the organization from within when the team dissolved. Instead they continued informally. What was different, however, was that they now had broader access to the resources and promotional energy necessary to get their ideas diffused. The outcome was a set of bold new products introduced to the market.

4. Disruption Connections

Adaptive Space enables connections to overcome the stifling effects of formal structure and facilitates network closure—that is, the spreading of an idea through an organization where key influencers are more likely to hear about it. Formalization is the final step in agility, representing the endorsement of new solutions into the formal operational system. This can also be the hardest stage. Within traditional organizational structures and processes, formal leaders can act as a roadblock for new ideas and innovation. This should not be a surprise. The very nature of their role is to make strategic decisions about resource optimization—and as a result they are inundated with numerous ideas and suggestions daily, creating a natural propensity to be conservative. Because managers are not able to provide a favorable response to all of these requests (even the solid ideas), positive network buzz and more fully developed concepts become critical in determining which ideas get selected for implementation. This is the power of challenger interactions. Challengers disrupt existing structures to enable the ongoing consideration of new ideas.

Consider one of the many examples from our research study. Two financial service companies were in the midst of a major integration. The acquired company was much smaller than its parent organization and was known for its entrepreneurial spirit. The company encouraged active participation from its employees and operated as a tightly knit, family-like team. It had enjoyed tremendous success through a series of innovative products that were quickly introduced to the market. In contrast, the much larger parent company was a disciplined machine with a highly focused operational system. At first glance, the marriage felt like a disaster to the smaller entrepreneurial company. However, over time the disruptive interactions began to loosen up the power structures of the larger parent company. By deploying Adaptive Space, a series of local successes from the smaller company were morphed and modified so they would be considered for additional product lines by the parent company and then scaled across a vastly larger distribution channel. What initially seemed like a marriage doomed for failure ultimately became a catalyst for a series of resounding market successes.

Ideas that have been developed and iterated through pressure testing against critical risks are more likely to be supported by the operational system. It is rarely a wise thing to pitch an idea blindly to a leader. The formalization process is as much a social phenomenon as it is a business decision. Therefore, if an individual pitches an idea that has not generated social momentum, it is less likely to be considered. Network closure is thus another connection that enables both disruption and acceptance. Network closure is the closing in around a potential sponsor of information flowing across multiple networks. When it occurs, individuals begin to hear information from multiple sources, increasing the potential for the idea to attract notice, be heard, and gain support. Gossip, social ownership of an idea, and network closure allows ideas to amplify and spread, ultimately creating network buzz that can positively influence an operational leader to make the decision for formal endorsement.

Together, the 4D connections act as the fuel for agility. Adaptive Space can therefore be thought of as social interconnectivity that facilitates the active interplay of discovery, development, diffusion, and disruption. Perhaps it is best described as an organizational playground, much like that at a school recess. Children charge out from the various cohesive classrooms of study—mathematics, social studies, or art class—and engage in creative exchanges. Driven by energy and interest, children participate in semi-structured activities such as kickball, hopscotch, tag, or just good old-fashioned gossip. These interactions result in brokerage exchanges of children that come from the bridging of classroom clusters. The playground provides an opportunity for connecting based on common interest and passions. These exchanges also result in high-energy interactions as groups come together and feud over their differences. This is exactly what happens inside agile organizations. Adaptive Space provides the relational freedom for people to openly explore and exchange ideas. It enables connections so that people, ideas, information, and resources can be linked up for greater impact. Adaptive Space also enables the connections necessary for debate and disruptive interactions to emerge, often resulting in formal endorsement. The outcome is a generative energy that fuels agility.

Adapt or Die

Most organizations don't suffer from a deficit of ideas. Plenty of people have innovative and entrepreneurial ideas that can benefit the organization's ability to adapt and adjust. Ideas are cheap, and people are excited to share them. But we also know that when new ideas are offered, the most common response is to shut them down. People feel like they hit a brick wall when they present their ideas and are stopped in their tracks by those who don't want the change or who see too many obstacles. And unfortunately, this doesn't come just from managers—it occurs at all levels within the organization.

Organizations can't help themselves. They do what they are designed to do—they are set up to drive operational efficiencies. Although times have changed dramatically, many organizations struggle with change. They have doubled down on investing in advanced operational systems, focusing intensely on concepts like data analytics, machine learning, and artificial intelligence to strive for greater efficiency and order while underinvesting in creativity and agility. In fact, many of them have perfected the operational system at the expense of agility. And when we do this, we are exposing ourselves to tremendous risk. In today's environment, the old adage is increasingly true: *adapt or die*.

Adaptive Space is the answer. It is the key marker of agile organizations. To enable Adaptive Space and make organizations more agile, we need to leverage certain types of interactions that promote and support the 4D connections of Adaptive Space. In the chapters that follow, *Adaptive Space* will consider ways to do just this. This book is broken into two primary parts. The first part focuses on explaining the 4D connections of Adaptive Space by first highlighting the discovery and development potential of brokers and connecters respectively. It goes on to illustrate the power of energizers and challengers in facilitating diffusion and disruption. The second part of the book outlines five easy-to-remember principles necessary to open up Adaptive Space within any organization: Engage the Edges, Find a Friend, Follow the Energy, Embrace the Conflict, and Close the Network.

2

• ———————————— •

Discovery Connections of Brokers

Creativity is just connecting things.

—STEVE JOBS

I n February of 1995 Lawrence Levy became the new CFO of Pixar. When he arrived everyone was friendly, welcoming him and politely indicating they were glad he was there. But something wasn't right. Pixar had been described to him as a fun, family-like environment, but Levy sensed that the people around him were being aloof. It didn't take long to find out why. While having a conversation with Pam Kerwin, vice president at Pixar, she said, "I don't envy you . . . I don't think you really get what you're up against." Levy was confused. "Up against?" he asked. Kerwin's response was, "You're Steve's guy."[1]

The Steve she was referring to was Steve Jobs. When Levy joined Pixar, Jobs was the primary investor, and his relationship with the company was tumultuous. According to Kerwin: "Steve is the guy who owns us—but he's never been one of us."[2]

The Pixar team feared Jobs. They worried that he didn't understand what they did and that he would ruin Pixar by destroying the culture. The problem for Levy was that everyone believed Jobs had sent him in to fix the company, and there was little doubt the company needed fixing. Pixar had been in business for 10 years and was not making money. Jobs himself had invested close to $50 million yet was still covering the company's monthly cash shortfall. But the early Pixar employees nevertheless felt betrayed by Jobs. He had committed to providing them with stock options, as is typical for Silicon Valley start-ups, and in their minds he hadn't proved himself trustworthy because he had not yet fulfilled this commitment.

Levy was in a difficult situation. He needed to bridge two groups with different views. As CFO he understood Jobs's concerns more clearly than most. Yet he also heard the Pixar employees and empathized with them. He agreed that the option plan was fundamental to propelling the company forward, and he appreciated that the employees were still thinking "big" and wanted to be beneficiaries of Pixar's grand success. On the other hand, he also learned that Jobs had promised a handful of Pixar's senior executives a share of Pixar's film profits that might be converted into stock options, while leaving others out. Levy knew this could be disastrous. If one of the more influential employees became frustrated enough to leave, it could trigger an exodus of Pixar's talent. And all this coincided with the planned release of *Toy Story*.

Levy knew he had to act quickly to find a solution that would work for both sides. If he was to be successful, he needed to bridge this divide and get everyone focused on the launch of *Toy Story*. To do this, he first had to convince Jobs that the options issue was critically important to the future success of

Pixar—certainly not an easy task as Jobs was annoyed about continuing to fund a losing business. However, after much give-and-take, Levy was able to convince Jobs to revise his views and release some funding for options. This alleviated a major concern for the employees. Levy and the leadership team were then able to shift focus toward two major milestones: the release of *Toy Story* and Pixar's IPO. His efforts paid off. Both happened in the same week in November of 1995. *Toy Story* went on to be a smash hit, grossing $365 million in global box office sales alone. The IPO was similarly successful. On November 29, 1995, the company's stocks were offered to the public at $22 a share, closing the day at $39, and valuing Pixar at $1.5 billion.[3]

The Insight of Brokers

Lawrence Levy acted as a broker. His efforts were essential in finding and enabling a solution that allowed Pixar to become an icon in computer animation films. Brokers provide bridge connections across groups. They link groups and individuals to one another. This uniquely positions them to capitalize on opportunities requiring the integration of different perspectives. For example, as a broker Levy was able to build political support. He wasn't the most connected individual within the organization. However, he was the best-positioned person to deeply understand the political dynamics. Therefore he was able to navigate through the differences and discover a solution that was amenable to both parties. Levy had unique insight about the situation.

To be successful, brokers recognize they should not limit their interactions to those in their primary work group. Rather, they reach out and engage people in other teams and organizations.

These connections help them to better understand what is going on. And because of their brokerage connections, they come to understand political dynamics, develop greater proficiency, and discover trends happening both within and outside the organization. Their position in the network enables them to be culturally sensitive, enhancing their ability in coordinating efforts among people with competing perspectives. The result is that they are highly capable to act as translators, conveying information from one group to another about what is most important and why.

Brokers foster discovery connections that enhance the flow of ideas, insights, and information within and across an organization. They are critical in overcoming *insularity*— the overwhelming tendency of groups to become isolated and inwardly focused. We call these insular groups silos. Insularity limits agility by locking people into a comfort zone of complacency. When this happens, individuals become overly influenced by the people within their primary circle of influence—people with similar skills, experiences, and mindsets—and dismissive of others holding different views. Silos severely limit the ability of the organization to be agile. Brokers help overcome this by creating connections that forge linkages and promote discovery. We know, for example, that ideas are triggered at the intersection of networks or entrepreneurial pockets. When two diverse groups connect, the potential for novelty increases. For example, in one pharmaceutical company the innovation process could be traced to a few key scientists who were brokers to outside academics. When two of these brokers left the organization, critical relationships were lost. The result was a significant decline in the innovation rate for the company.

Sociologist Ron Burt suggests that brokers make their contributions by offering three competitive advantages to an organization.[4] First, through their outreach, brokers provide broader access to diverse information. They have relationships across heterogeneous groups and can bridge silos to generate new insights and act as a gateway for new ideas. Second, because they are connected in ways that give them access to trends in the environment and the organization, they provide early access to new information. Their connections allow them to be "in the know" about new developments both inside and outside the organization. Third, because brokers are accessing the information, they also have control over how they use it. This offers them a critical source of power, as they can determine whether, when, and how information is released and diffused. When brokers leave, as we saw in the example above with the pharmaceutical company, the insights and connections they bring to the organization can leave with them.

Brokers play an essential role in opening up Adaptive Space. They represent the bridge connections from one entrepreneurial pocket to another. These bridges provide access to new insights and discoveries from outside the entrepreneurial pocket by providing connections to novel ideas and diverse perspectives. As a result, ideas are linked up to create the potential for bolder outcomes. Just consider for a moment where new ideas come from. Generally speaking, when we are engaged in our day-to-day routine, we are plodding along for incremental changes. Yet, when we step outside of our daily confines, insight strikes. This is often the result of brokerage, even if not in the moment. We connect one thing to another, and we have a new perspective. Insight emerges. Adaptive Space encourages these connections.

Traditionally, within organizations, brokerage has occurred as a result of personal interest or responsibility. For example, curious individuals may connect to another group in the spirit of learning something new, or a scientist might forge a specific research relationship with a university to stay current. However, in most organizations this is left to chance. Making this even more challenging is the fact that the operational system pulls people toward daily performance and therefore doesn't value brokerage connections, leaving little free time for individuals to reach out beyond their local team. The result is greater insularity as people limit interactions to those who help them deliver on day-to-day performance. This is why Adaptive Space is so critical. It helps to facilitate deliberate discovery connections. It capitalizes on the benefits of brokerage by creating opportunities for individuals to connect more actively with others beyond their current silos and explore new possibilities.

A good example of creating discovery connections through Adaptive Space is what MasterCard Labs does. MasterCard Labs was founded in 2012 with the intention of being an internal disruptor to its core business.[5] It was designed to intentionally connect global employees with one another and harness their diverse backgrounds, experiences, and perspectives, thereby enabling greater brokerage. One of the more popular programs from Labs is the Innovation Express, which brings together teams of developers, designers, and a variety of other business-people around a given challenge. Multiple products and services have been generated from the Innovation Express method. One of the more interesting products is Qkr! (pronounced "quicker"). MasterCard Labs sponsored a challenge designed to think about a "world beyond cash." It then invited people from across various teams to come together in the New York lab to focus on this challenge. Forty-eight hours later, employees came up with a smartphone payment app idea and numerous use cases to pitch it. The concept enabled consumers to order and pay in advance for products and services using a smartphone. For example, one application helped eliminate the waiting lines at stadiums where fans could use Qkr! to order food delivered directly to their seats or to be picked up in an express line. Another application enabled parents to order their kids' school lunches in advance and pay without cash. Today, Qkr! can be seen in restaurants as a quick service system that provides customers a choice to skip waiting by preordering and paying for their food.

Qkr! is a great illustration of discovery in action. When organizations are challenged to think beyond their day-to-day operational boundaries, new ideas emerge. Agility begins with discovery connections—the triggering of ideas, new insights, and learning that lead to alternative ways of thinking and creating in an organization. Silos or insularity inhibit the discovery process, which prevents individuals from connecting to generate novel ideas. Adaptive Space is needed to encourage and enable individuals to navigate beyond their local groups. Adaptive Space helps to unleash the insight of brokers by intentionally harnessing the latent potential that exists from diverse backgrounds, experiences, and perspectives. The result is an organization that is more agile and poised to positively disrupt itself.

Connecting the Discovery Dots

When we look at the success of Apple over the past decade and a half, it is easy to suggest that it is the result of visionary leadership and brilliant design. From the outside in, it seems as if Apple is the most insular company on planet Earth. Just consider the development of the first iPod. Apple is infamous for its ability to develop under a shroud of secrecy. The iPod team consisted of about 25 employees working in isolation in one of the remote buildings on campus. As a result, when the iPod was released in October 2001, very few people knew about it. The truth is that Apple continues to operate within a cloud of secrecy today, using speculation and rumors to its own benefit. When we dig a little deeper, however, another story begins to emerge. While Apple is composed of clearly identifiable network clusters of inventors and related technology specialists, these entrepreneurial pockets are actually connected by a handful of critical brokers who facilitate the discovery process.

After his experience with Lawrence Levy at Pixar, Jobs reentered Apple for round two with a different perspective. Jobs took advantage of his exile from Apple to develop his network in Silicon Valley. During this time Jobs was a masterful broker. He was known for working the phones. He called people if he heard they were involved in something interesting. He requested meetings to discuss ideas or pitch an opportunity. Jobs spent much of his time outside Apple working the Silicon Valley ecosystem. As his legend grew, no one would turn down the chance to meet with him. He could summon the best young entrepreneurs on a day's notice. Each of these interactions was an opportunity to discover something new. Jobs was able to establish critical connections, placing him on the edge of the most interesting discoveries. While he is credited as the demanding visionary who changed the way the world lives, his true brilliance may have been the result of his ability to act as a broker. His knack to gather insights from a diverse range of interesting people and perspectives allowed him to envision new possibilities well before others could. Jobs's genius was his ability to quickly synthesize discoveries from his network. This aptitude emerged as the result of access to diverse, novel information.

His seemingly supernatural understanding of market needs and technological advancements was not a fluke, but rather a result of his brokerage position, whereby ultimately it was his network that did much of the work!

We can see evidence of Jobs's brokerage within the ranks of Apple as well. Researcher André Vermeij analyzed the network of patents linked to Apple between 1978 and 2014.[6] What Vermeij found is fascinating. A mere 19 patents were published during the first decade of Apple's existence. By 2014 that number exploded to more than 9,600 patents. When Jobs first reentered the company, he played only a marginal role in the patent network. Between 2002 and 2007, however, this changed significantly. During this time an elaborate internal network of patents emerged. Discovery connections between the Industrial Design team, the User Interface group, and the iTunes organization began to solidify. Fundamental to all of this, however, was Steve Jobs. He positioned himself as the primary gatekeeper between these groups. In Figure 2.1, Jobs can be seen as the central broker as the large, dark dot in the center of Apple's patent ecosystem. He was an expert at drawing intelligence out of his network. Jobs followed his curiosity and served as a broker to discover new things—he actively asked questions of others and engaged in many interests. This curiosity drove him to pay attention to the world around him and to seek out diverse groups of people with a wide range of ideas, both inside and outside of Apple.

He also had a tremendous ability to take these ideas and synthesize them to create incredible new innovations. Perhaps his most famous quote is, "You can't connect the dots looking forward; you can only connect them looking backwards. So you have to trust that the dots will somehow connect in your future."

While there is no doubt Jobs was a visionary and a brilliant strategist, it was his network that did much of the work that empowered his brilliance.

FIGURE 2.1 Steve Jobs as a Broker

Used with permission from André Vermeij of Kenedict Innovation Analytics

---

Jobs had a distinctive ability to connect the discovery dots. In 2002, Apple was an unprofitable, struggling computer company with one seemingly novel success, the music-playing iPod. However, by the time of Jobs's premature death in 2011, Apple had grown into a technological powerhouse with an entire ecosystem of inventors. And Jobs had positioned himself to act as the primary broker, able to quickly activate any part of the network in response to market needs.

Brokerage facilitates the discovery process through the generation of creativity and the flow of novel ideas. Jobs was able to create bridge connections between groups and act as a critical link within the network. He benefited from the competitive advantages of brokers. He had wider access to diverse information, he had early access to new information, and perhaps most important, he controlled the flow of the information. The result was a generative conduit of fresh ideas and innovations that enabled Apple to be agile.

Bridges to the Next Big Thing

Research suggests that individuals who are connected to a broad external network of experts have greater access to innovative ideas. As a result, many companies have adopted innovation-scouting programs focused on establishing and nurturing external discovery connections. However, this is only part of the solution. Researchers Linus Dahlander and Siobhan O'Mahony studied what is called the "variance hypothesis" to better understand the benefits of these programs.[7] The variance hypothesis suggests that a broad set of external connections leads to better innovation outcomes. The researchers were interested in validating this hypothesis, so they examined the innovation outcomes of more than 660 senior technical experts from IBM who were formally responsible for scouting new ideas. The primary responsibility of these experts was to figure out what would be the next big thing for IBM. They operated with high degrees of autonomy to search for new ideas. Dahlander and O'Mahony collected data to comprehensively understand where each of these experts spent their time. They then compared these results to the innovation outcomes that were generated.

What they discovered was surprising. Individuals who focused most of their attention on building internal brokerage connections were actually quite innovative. While external discovery connections were important, internal brokerage seemed to be equally critical. When you think about it, this makes sense. Steve Jobs was successful because he acted as both an internal and external broker. If people spend too much time searching for external ideas, there is no time available to engage internal colleagues. They actually risk being marginalized by the internal network, often being accused of being too theoretical or impractical. Building internal social capital enables these brokers to more readily share their discoveries. Additionally, as we saw with Lawrence Levy, these connections are also indispensable in uncovering internal solutions. While external brokers are essential to discovering new ideas, internal brokers are crucial to driving application within entrepreneurial pockets.

Consider the analogy of a structural bridge across a river. Civil engineers spend much of their time designing the abutment on both ends of the bridge span. Each side must be intentionally designed for the bridge to be effective. The substructures at the ends of a given span are essential. They provide structural support for the bridge. Abutments transfer the load of the bridge span to the foundation. The same is true for brokerage bridges. If they are only connected on one side, they become unstable. For external discovery connections to be effective, they must be supported by solid internal connections, or the new learning cannot be distributed into the network. This is how external ideas are seeded into the network.

Not all new ideas come from outside. Lateral bridge connections between internal entrepreneurial pockets are also critical to discovery. These lateral interactions from pocket to pocket are particularly rich in organizations that are siloed. More often than not, solutions to a problem or new insights have already been discovered. They are just unevenly distributed. Lateral discovery connections help with this. They provide the internal conduit for these ideas, insights, and learning to flow more smoothly across an organization. Just as with external brokers, internal brokers can be quickly dismissed by their own local team if they don't spend enough time engaging in team development. Lateral connections must also forge solid abutments on both sides of the bridge.

In most organizations internal brokers aren't the senior leaders like Steve Jobs sitting at the top of the organizational chart. They are also not necessarily the top experts in their domain, as they were in the IBM example. Rather, they connect experts and leaders across the firm. Brokers actively navigate across boundaries and enable Adaptive Space by bringing people together who are otherwise not connected. Brokers laterally span entrepreneurial pockets to generate new possibilities. For example, in one research case a junior marketing professional was interested in a new digital design platform. When he presented his idea to a member of the senior marketing team, it was cursorily dismissed. However, the young marketing professional was so convinced of the benefits of the new solution that he decided to share it with young professionals on other teams. One of these professionals discovered that the new platform featured capabilities that alleviated a major migration problem. It helped him to automate a very manual data transfer. He quickly began to showcase this solution to his local team, and they too realized the value. As a result, the entire marketing department, even those who were initially dismissive, adopted the solution. The junior marketing professional bridged the pockets of disparate entrepreneurial teams. As a result, he was able to trigger new insights that led to a new solution. This is how innovation generally spreads; it is rarely declared from the top or the result of a single-minded expert. More often than not, it is the result of someone acting as a broker who bridges entrepreneurial pockets.

Researchers from the Kellogg School of Management at Northwestern University show that the geniuses of yesterday, responsible for such scientific breakthroughs as the Heisenberg uncertainty principle, Euclidean geometry, and Nash's equilibrium theory, are now giving way to collaborative scholars working together through brokerage across entrepreneurial pockets. Led by Brian Uzzi, the research team searched 19.9 million published papers and more than 2.1 million patents over the past few decades to analyze the power of co-authorship across groups.[8] Their findings demonstrate that science has been shifting in a remarkably fundamental way. Over the past 45 years, the average number of authors on a given research paper has grown steadily from 1.9 to 3.5. These authors often bridge across disciplines, departments, and even universities. Furthermore, Uzzi and his colleagues discovered that the papers with multiple authors are cited twice as often as those written by a single individual. They also determined that the so-called "home-run papers," publications with at least a hundred citations, are six times as likely to come from multiple researchers. It is the richness of bridging connections across diverse groups that enables discovery.

It is true that brokerage often spurs new insights as entrepreneurial pockets are bridged. However, the tension generated in the collision of perspectives from pocket to pocket is also incredibly valuable, often resulting in morphed ideas that emerge from this sort of pressure testing. Competing needs and conflicting priorities spark creative thinking and challenge groups to come up with new possibilities. If everyone has the same perspective, there is no pressure to identify alternative solutions. Brokerage connections enable Adaptive Space so people, ideas, information, and resources can be linked up in new, creative combinations. Adaptive Space allows individuals to freely navigate beyond their local subgroups and actively interact with entrepreneurial pockets to explore new possibilities.

A great organizational example of this was the development of the Motorola Razr. When the Razr was first introduced in 2004, it shattered a few cell phone paradigms. It was the world's first thin phone that sported an illuminated keypad made out of a single metal wafer. The Razr was artfully elegant, with a hidden antenna, and functionally impressive with a high-powered camera. It was also remarkably successful, selling a breathtaking 12.5 million units in less than a year. What most people don't know is that the Razr also had to break some internal rules.[9] To stimulate bolder outcomes, Motorola enabled physical Adaptive Space to more intentionally bridge entrepreneurial pockets. Engineers were challenged to leave the comfort of their cubicles in their research and development facility and move into a downtown Chicago innovation lab where they worked side by side with designers and marketers on the Razr. Everyone was positioned to act as a broker, and the space fostered daily clashes, debates, and discoveries across these normally divided groups. The outcome of these entrepreneurial pockets being thrust together through Adaptive Space solutions was that the broker quotient of the organization was increased, allowing the breakthrough product, the Razr, to be developed. However, brokerage connections are also critical beyond organizational boundaries.

Enabling Adaptive Space in Ecosystems

Tel Aviv is the hub of a rich entrepreneurial network that has helped Israel emerge as a start-up powerhouse. The country ranks as one of the most robust start-up ecosystems in the world. It holds claim to success statistics that other countries can only envy and has the largest number of start-ups per capita in the world. It has more companies listed on the NASDAQ than Europe, Japan, Korea, India, and China combined. It also leads the world in the number of researchers per capita, which has led to a high-density technology hub that launches, attracts, and develops a multitude of high-tech companies and R&D centers of multinational corporations.

The Israeli government, venture capital firms, corporations, and the Israel Defense Forces' (IDF) Elite Technological Units have all worked together to enable this capacity by creating a rich ecosystem of Adaptive Space for start-ups to emerge. In 1974 the Israeli government commissioned the Office of the Chief Scientist (since renamed the Israeli Innovation Authority) with a dedicated fund for research and development. Today the government supports a multitude of incubator programs and provides grant funding to such domains as heavy tech, clean tech, and medical devices.

Perhaps most important, the government has instilled a culture of innovation across the country by creating Adaptive Space that encourages experimentation, failure, and entrepreneurialism. Israel boasts a rich venture capital industry that offers the world's highest per capita availability of funding. Corporations have also stepped in, opening R&D centers and innovation accelerators. Nearly 100 accelerators and incubators operate within Tel Aviv, including corporate-sponsored programs from such companies as Microsoft, Google, and Citi. The Microsoft Accelerator selects some of the highest potential start-ups every year and enables them to develop go-to-market and product strategies. Moreover, the IDF's Elite Technological Units have acted as a training base of entrepreneurship. Mandatory enlistment for all Israelis provides access to a wide array of development opportunities. It provides a nonhierarchical Adaptive Space where creativity and intelligence are cultivated.

With such a rich interaction of partners working together for a common purpose, it is no wonder such a vibrant ecosystem has emerged. At the core of this Adaptive Space is the brokerage capacity of Unit 8200—a unit formed in response to Israel's need for national security. The 8200 is an Israeli Intelligence Corps unit responsible for collecting intelligence signals and decrypting code within the Israeli Defense Forces. It is a special tech unit within the army that conscripts the best and the brightest men and women and trains them in cutting-edge military technology. It is also the incubator of thousands of Israeli entrepreneurs, where high-potential candidates are scouted at an early age from across the nation's high schools.

The military looks for students with social skills, analytic abilities, and future potential. Over the next few years these 18-year-olds are exposed to advanced technological challenges and empowered to work together in teams. They study advanced machine learning and data-mining techniques and explore highly advanced technologies. They also engage in real-world defense simulations, forcing them to take risks and make mistakes. They are challenged to work together and given the autonomy to bypass army hierarchies when necessary. The result is a set of technologically skilled, deeply connected entrepreneurial leaders who have created such companies as CheckPoint,

Waze, and Wix. In fact, Forbes estimates that the 8200 alumni have founded more than 1,000 companies. As it turns out, tracking terrorists translates well to tracking consumers. The Unit 8200 members spend their time in the forces exploring highly advanced technologies, and these learnings translate well into commercial uses. Additionally, the strong relationships forged while operating in the unit keep alumni connected so that they can deftly employ the benefits of brokerage. The deep bonds formed by working closely together also generate future brokerage capacity for the 8200 alumni, as they are able to check in with old colleagues to evaluate, discuss, and discover ideas.

Perhaps this is best illustrated with Inbal Arieli, who served in the 8200 in the late 1990s.[10] She served five years as a lieutenant in the elite intelligence unit, overseeing the office's training school. *Forbes* magazine describes Arieli as the "Connector," building bridges between entrepreneurs, start-ups, and companies across the Israeli innovation and tech ecosystem. She founded numerous programs for innovators, including Israel's first start-up accelerator, GAMMADO, a tech talent incubator, and the 8200 EISP, an Adaptive Space that harnesses the vast network of the 8200 alumni to enable early-stage entrepreneurs to grow their businesses through an intensive yearlong program. Arieli's ability to create Adaptive Space that links ideas, initiatives, and resources has helped her to become one of the 100 Most Influential People in Israeli high tech, and one of the 100 most popular tech businesswomen speakers in the world. She has worked closely with many Israeli start-ups and has acted as an executive member and advisor to several high-tech companies and start-ups. She also frequently provides guidance and mentorship to a variety of emerging start-up ecosystems in other countries, such as South Korea, Bulgaria, France, and

Switzerland. Arieli has positioned herself as a broker inside of a vibrant ecosystem. As a result she is able to quickly identify interesting connections, create new opportunities for greater impact, and leverage Adaptive Space through her relationships in order to connect individuals for discovery.

Ecosystem and Organizational Convergence

Broker benefits don't just work across an ecosystem. They can also have a significant impact within an organization. Gil Golan is the director of General Motors' Advanced Technical Center in Israel (ATC-I). He is also a graduate of Unit 8200 and a broker. Golan is hyperconnected across both the Tel Aviv ecosystem and General Motors. He is constantly nurturing, establishing, and leveraging relationships. Golan has established both internal and external abutment structures to support the ATC-I. He operates by the simple notion that you must establish relationships before you need them, frequently checking in with others to understand their needs and discuss possibilities. Golan operates well beyond his technical center bubble and views himself more as an ambassador for mobility than the director of a center. As an example, during a yearlong company-sponsored development program for senior executives, Golan actively built his relationship network, moving from the fringe of the network to a primary position of a cross-functional, multiregional group of senior executives. He had effectively migrated from being relatively unknown to some critical players to becoming a go-to person in the tech arena. As a result, he is able to forge bridges through senior executives to such groups as engineering, public policy, marketing, and planning.

Golan also recognizes that building an Advanced Technical Center involves forming a team of highly skilled, creative individuals who understand the significant challenges of mobility. As Golan states: "What we are developing today in Israel could contribute to and influence the future of transportation, lifestyle, and culture generally."[11] The GM Advanced Technical Center in Israel was established with a clear vision of hiring the most qualified and brightest talent in order to excel on cutting-edge, nontraditional automotive technologies. The technical domains and ongoing work streams include software and hardware groups that work on the most complex challenges facing the new mobility era. The center develops cutting-edge technologies that are shaping the future of mobility by focusing on such things as smart sensing, signal processing, sensor fusion, and cognitive systems.

Golan recognizes the importance of brokering relationships to make this happen. He has been instrumental in coordinating R&D work with governments, leading institutions, national laboratories, high-tech companies, and global industrial partners. Golan helped facilitate an agreement with Israel's Ministry of Transport to provide GM with a permit to test autonomous vehicle technologies on Israel's roads. Like Inbal Arieli, Golan also recognizes the power of the 8200 alumni as a vital connective fabric to enable mobility advancement. As he observes, "I see the integration of the unit's graduates as an important advantage over other companies."[12]

The GM Advanced Technical Center also facilitates Adaptive Space events to enable brokerage across the Israel ecosystem. On April 25, 2017, the center sponsored a self-driving car hackathon to the broader ecosystem. Technology lovers, researchers, and algorithm developers were invited to bring their talent, passions, and determination to engage in a challenge. During the day of the event, several hundred people showed up to participate. The challenge was presented in the morning, and participants worked in predetermined teams for the next 48 hours. The center provided food, large floor pillows for necessary naps, and mentoring from 25 GM cognitive driving team engineers. At the conclusion of the hackathon, each team presented its solution for a virtual driver. Advanced features and the ability to adequately fulfill safety requirements were also evaluated. Gil Golan led the judging panel, and the winning team won a trip to the 2018 Consumer Electronics Show (CES) in Las Vegas. Perhaps most important, GM forged several hundred connections for discovery. Facilitating the convergence of the Tel Aviv ecosystem with the GM Advanced Technical Center enabled Adaptive Space.

Crafting Discovery Connections

Brokers enable Adaptive Space by creating the discovery connections necessary to allow ideas, information, and learning to flow more openly. They are uniquely positioned, providing them with critical insight to accurately understand political dynamics and find solutions for competing perspectives. Brokers are also critical in overcoming insularity by providing the bridge connections from one entrepreneurial pocket to another. These bridges provide access to novel ideas and diverse perspectives that challenge others to engage beyond the day-to-day routine. There are five essential ways to facilitate discovery connections.

1. **Intentionally place brokers in position.** Organizations need to position individuals to navigate between diverse teams, enabling them to capitalize on opportunities

that require the integration of different perspectives and increase the flow of insights. These brokers are able to better understand political dynamics throughout the organization so they can act as translators, conveying information from one group to another.

2. **Increase brokerage interactions.** Brokerage is critical in overcoming insularity. Organizations need to enable brokerage to fully leverage their advantages of having broader access to diverse information and gaining early access to novel ideas. They also need to challenge brokers to openly share and distribute their insights in the most useful manner.

3. **Facilitate discovery activities.** Organizations need to create deliberate discovery connections. They need to facilitate discovery events and cross-team exchanges similar to MasterCard's Innovation Express. They need to intentionally exploit the diverse perspectives and expertise that exist within the organizations, therefore connecting the discovery dots.

4. **Build bridges across pockets.** Organizations need to create conduits for fresh ideas and innovations. They need to ensure a balanced approach to creating external discovery connections with internal brokerage to drive application in entrepreneurial pockets. They need to challenge individuals to more actively connect and navigate beyond their local subgroups.

5. **Create convergence.** Organizations need to build discovery connections with external brokers to gain greater access to ecosystem insights. They need to sponsor events similar to the GM Advanced Technical Center hackathon to attract external brokers.

Brokers create the discovery connections that enact Adaptive Space within an organization. The result is that people, information, resources, and technology can be combined into new solutions, positioning an organization to become more agile.

3

•————————•

Development Interactions of Connectors

It's their "ideas" that appeal to me.
I am quite correctly described as more
of a sponge than an inventor.

—THOMAS EDISON

I n late 1875 Thomas Edison bought 34 rural acres in Raritan Township, New Jersey, in order to build a groundbreaking research lab, Menlo Park. Over the next decade, the location turned into Edison's "Invention Factory," generating more than 400 patents. At its peak, Menlo Park occupied more than two square city blocks and included a laboratory, a glass house, a carpenters' shop, a carbon shed, and a blacksmith shop. Edison's Invention Factory provided the world with the phonograph, a practical incandescent light, a carbon microphone, an electric generator, and the first electric power distribution system. Through such marvelous inventions and their impact on changing people's lives, Edison became known as the "Wizard of

Menlo Park." The campus operated as a small industrial city, housing nearly all conceivable materials and equipment necessary to develop ideas into various groundbreaking inventions. Edison believed that imagination helped to generate ideas, but that technical knowledge and experimentation brought them into the world.

Behind the wizard, however, was a team of resourceful engineers and master tradesmen who acted as clockmakers, machinists, and glassblowers. These individuals worked long hours tinkering, building, testing, and refining ideas, for the magic of Menlo Park was not actually in the discovery of new ideas: it was in the improvement and optimization of existing ideas to make them less expensive and more robust for consumer use. Most of the patents generated were enhancements of existing ideas, resulting from long hours of tenacious work and development from a cohesive group of what Edison affectionately dubbed the "muckers."[1] Edison may have been recognized as the Wizard of Menlo Park, but he was actually the central connector of a cohesive group of muckers.

Edison was brilliant at attracting young talent from around the world and assembling small cohesive teams. He depended on them to build and test ideas. At any point in time, multiple small teams were working on different products or concepts. Edison's muckers worked very closely with one another for long durations, developing and perfecting solutions and building camaraderie. When they weren't at work they were drinking, smoking, or eating together at Sarah Jordan's boarding house. Projects often took years, resulting in strong connections and cohesive teams that relied on each other. The environment was at times described as "coarse," with muckers challenging one another to move faster or try harder, but they could do this because they had established a level of trust that allowed them to feel safe even when they were aggressive with one another. In short, they forged strong development connections.

In 1878, Edison announced to the world that he had made an incandescent light. The world was so fascinated that the stock price of gas companies dropped immediately. There was one problem, however. Edison's current concept for the light bulb was not yet market viable. Over the next year, the muckers went to work. They tested more than 3,000 designs for bulbs, experimenting with various parts of the light bulb, such as a better vacuum pump, cables, and generators to make it more practical. One mucker, Charles Batchelor, or "Batch," with a reputation for being versatile and having good mechanical sense, tested one thing after another to create a long-lasting filament that glowed inside a light bulb.[2] He tested everything from linen, to wood, to rubber. At the same time, Ludwig Boehm from Germany carefully blew the glass and perfected the ideal design for the bulb, while John Kruesi from Switzerland designed the dynamo that would generate the electric power necessary for a series of light bulbs. After thousands of experiments, Edison and the muckers determined that a small, carbonized cotton thread was their best solution. They placed it inside a perfectly designed glass tube and carefully vacuumed out the air and sealed the bulb. Months of experimentation finally paid off when their light bulb was complete and able to burn for a whopping total of 13 hours.

In November of 1879, another mucker by the name of Francis Upton, or "Culture" as he was affectionately nicknamed by Edison for his piano-playing talent and impeccable educational credentials, wrote a letter saying, "The electric light is coming." To showcase the invention, a public demonstration was scheduled for New Year's Eve. Visitors were invited to Menlo Park to see the laboratory, the grounds, and 100 new lamps that illuminated Sarah Jordan's boarding house. The public was astonished. However, Edison and the muckers weren't finished. Several months later they determined that a carbonized bamboo filament could burn for more than 1,200 hours. They also continued to work on the broader electrical power system. In 1882, Edison fitted all the buildings on Pearl Street in Menlo Park with about 400 incandescent bulbs and hundreds of people gathered to witness the monumental breakthrough—an entire street lit with electricity.

Thomas Edison may be known as the Wizard of Menlo Park, and he certainly took credit for all of the 400-plus patents generated, but his reputation as a brilliant inventor, scientist, or even genius was more the result of his public displays. In reality, he was the central connector of a cohesive team of muckers.

Connectors Spur Development

While brokers are outstanding at finding ideas, they are not always positioned to influence their application. Discovery alone is insufficient without idea development and refinement. Ideas are cheap. To be useful, they must be applied. Harvard researcher Lee Fleming analyzed data from 35,400 collaborative inventors and found that while brokerage aids in the generation of an idea, it can actually hamper application.[3] Brokers do not have the cohesive relationships necessary for development. However, by engaging both brokers and connectors, generation and development are increased substantially. To be applied, ideas need to be socialized, tested, and iterated. This occurs best deep within entrepreneurial pockets, much in the same manner as with Edison's muckers. Central to the development process are connectors who forge cohesive relationships.

The two primary aspects of social capital are crucial to enabling Adaptive Space: brokerage and group cohesion. While brokers provide bridges to create a breadth of relationships, connectors nurture cohesive relationships of deep trust. Group cohesion represents how connected any given individual within a group is to others within the group. Highly cohesive groups have many redundant connections. That is, everyone is connected to everyone else. The benefit of cohesive groups is that individuals are able to quickly share information with one another. They also demonstrate higher levels of local trust. Often the result of cohesion is small, fertile entrepreneurial pockets of activity buried deep within the organization. The combination of brokerage and cohesion provides both access to diverse, novel ideas and the local trust necessary to build, test, and iterate ideas.

Agility in a social context requires a thorough understanding of the interplay between brokers and connectors. This is why Adaptive Space is so critical: it helps position individuals within the network structures to drive progress. Consider Hewlett-Packard, an organization whose name was once synonymous with innovation. In its glory days HP fostered a work environment that encouraged flexibility and innovation. The organization knew that in a technical business, with a rapid rate of progress, employees had to adapt. In those days, common practice was to hire an employee into a major project and then dismiss him or her upon completion of the project. At HP, however, the policy was to move engineers between projects rather than dismiss them. The result was the brokerage of key learnings and technologies into new projects, which could then be reconfigured in new ways. As a senior engineer once described it, "I had to work in a single field for only two or three years and then, like magic, it was a whole new field—a paradise for creativity."[4] HP intuitively knew that if people moved around, information would flow more readily, and it provided the space that enabled an active interplay between brokers and connectors.

Connectors help create entrepreneurial pockets that allow ideas to develop and take on life. The "magic" of these development connections is the local support that provides a safe and creative environment for experimentation and iteration. Because connectors are well positioned to garner support from within a pocket, they can quickly mobilize and drive local application to create better ideas that can be developed and scaled. In the Edison lab, the muckers were clearly a cohesive group. They did everything together, creating an environment of safety and trust that enabled them to challenge one another without worrying about hurting one another's feelings. This allowed them to quickly share information to connect ideas across the group, and made them more willing to experiment and take risks, which are critical components of innovation.

As connecters are critical to the development of entrepreneurial pockets, Adaptive Space is critical to enabling development within them. Cohesive groups often operate in isolation from other teams and can become highly insular. We often see this with traditional research and development teams that work largely in isolation, holed up, inventing the next big thing. The problem with this approach is that these ideas are rarely adopted by the broader organization. Edison, as the central connector, and his muckers were certainly locked into an entrepreneurial pocket when developing the incandescent light. However, the Edison example is unique in that he sometimes acted as a broker, thus providing the Adaptive Space necessary for bold innovation. Perhaps Edison said it best himself: "It's their 'ideas' that appeal to me. I am quite correctly described as more of a sponge than an inventor." Edison had a unique ability to absorb the ideas of others, be it as a connector with the muckers or as a broker combing through the patents of others. Additionally, Menlo Park itself enabled Edison to serve in a brokerage role in that it was set up to showcase the lab's inventions to the media.

Edison's true brilliance was therefore his ability to enable Adaptive Space that focused on the discovery of ideas, the development of those ideas, and then the diffusion of those ideas into the world. He intuitively knew when he needed to work beyond his cohesive network of muckers and when he needed to create discovery connections as a broker in the larger patent network. Yet, he was also agile, shifting focus toward nurturing development connections and providing a safe space for the muckers to build, experiment, and iterate their concepts. Finally, he was able to play in the pressures by showcasing his inventions before they were ready for real-world application. Edison challenged his team to ensure they developed concepts that were viable for the market. And it worked. Through lots of experimentation and a clear understanding of the operational and market needs, they were able to generate a light bulb that was, for all intents and purposes, disruptive. Adaptive Space created an invention factory that not only developed a practical light bulb but also ushered in the world's first phonograph, a carbon microphone, an electric generator, and an electric power distribution, to name a few. Adaptive Space enables development connections to occur in the context of brokerage. It facilitates development connections, while also creating greater excitement in the outside world. The result is a set of bolder outcomes that are accessible far beyond the entrepreneurial pocket, enabling agility.

Connectors Forge Relationships

As we have discussed, connectors, especially those who are more central, are essential in the development process. They are perfectly positioned, as Edison so aptly noted about himself, to act as sponges, soaking up the ideas of those around them and then enabling a cohesive team to build, test, and refine ideas as needed. Connectors are well positioned to garner support from within a given group. They can quickly drive local application, experimentation, and iteration, all of which enable the learning and refinement needed for development.

Central connectors also forge relationships and build strong ties. They do this by building reciprocity—they provide help to others that creates a "favor bank" they can call upon when needed. If the central connector does not know the answer, he or she usually knows who does, and has built the social capital that helps get a quick response. Central connectors are well situated in the network to drive local influencing, and the most effective central connectors are trusted, have credibility, and are willing to help. They make day-to-day work possible for many others and are critical when things go awry because they are often the first called on in crisis situations. As a result they become the go-to people in challenging times—often acting as the linchpin in getting things done.

Network expert Rob Cross from Babson College has been studying hundreds of organizational networks for over two decades. He describes central connectors as the individuals most frequently contacted for information, for expertise, and for making critical decisions. They are the most connected people in an organization. Cross's research suggests that somewhere between 3 and 5 percent of people in an organizational network represent between 20 and 35 percent of the valuable connections.[5] These people are essential to driving responsiveness. For example, in an oil industry organization, Cross found central engineers, geoscientists, and drillers were the most frequently contacted during unexpected challenges with oil wells, and central programmers were the most critical to problem solving when a computer system shut down. Additionally, these connectors are not just more capable of responding with answers to a crisis themselves, but they also have direct access to a vibrant set of experts around them.

For the past decade or more, organizations have dedicated much of their efforts to optimizing human capital strategies in an effort to win the war on talent—building comprehensive talent management systems, validating leadership competency models, and designing the best possible leadership development programs. In more recent years, however, emphasis has turned to enhancing employee engagement, refining performance management systems, and leveraging people analytics. While it is hard to argue against the need for these human capital–centric strategies, Adaptive Space challenges us to engage more in social capital strategies. It focuses on the competitive advantage that is created based on the way an individual is connected to others. Or as physicist Mark Buchanan says, "Social network specialists have been saying for years, beneath the formal organizational chart of any company lie hidden webs of social interactions that we rarely talk about."[6] Adaptive Space urges us to take a deeper look and more directly embrace these connections.

Connectors forge these relationships by providing a consistent track record of trust and credibility. Whereas brokers are outstanding at finding ideas, central connectors and the group cohesion they leverage play a critical role in getting things done. Connectors pick up where brokers leave off. They work beyond the formalities of human capital processes and advance concept development. They bring ideas to life.

Fierce Focus of "Two Pizza Teams"

As noted, for years society has glorified inventors. People like Leonardo da Vinci, Alexander Bell, and Thomas Edison have been elevated to hero status based on their astounding creations. However, a deeper look reveals a different reality. Social scientists Lee Fleming and Jasjit Singh have studied the lone inventors concept, and their findings are a bit surprising.[7] Rather than a lone inventor, invention is nearly always a result of collaboration. They argue that although lone inventors do exist, their inventions are not nearly as good as those of a group working in collaboration. The reality is that invention is usually a complex social process.

According to Fleming and Singh's findings, a small team was 64 percent more likely than a lone inventor to have a top 5 percent patent. Moreover, a small team was 28 percent less likely than a lone inventor to publish a poor patent. Lone inventors are, in fact, a myth. Nearly every marvelous creator is connected to a resourceful group of muckers. If we dive deeper into Apple's development model, we can see this in action. Steve Jobs was well positioned to act as a broker and discover bold new ideas. However, it was Apple's local development teams that were responsible for much of the actual creation. Jonathan Ive worked closely with Jobs on iMac design, introducing color and light into the drab world of computing. From that point forth, Ive's Industrial Design team worked as a small, close-knit team designing groundbreaking products such as the iPod, iPhone, MacBook Air, and iPad. The cohesive team of designers was a densely clustered group that represented nearly 20 percent of all Apple's patents between 2007 and 2012.

Apple's secretive initiative dubbed "Project Purple" challenged a small team, as an entrepreneurial pocket, to develop a computing system controlled by human touch without relying on extraneous hardware. The cohesive team developed a multi-touch user interface based on sensing screens into what we now know as the first iPhone. The development team spent countless hours perfecting such features as the slider to unlock the screen, the speed of scrolling, and placing calls directly from the address book. These small entrepreneurial pockets became the catalyst for a technological empire. According to one industrial designer at Apple, most of its products are initially conceived by a tightly connected group of just 15 or 16 designers—an inner circle of innovators. Researcher André Vermeij's mapping of Apple's patent network supports this claim, with 15 key inventors representing the core of 3,626 patents analyzed. In total, 98 Apple inventors were responsible for nearly 17 percent of all patents filed.[8]

Development is more fluid in a small, entrepreneurial pocket of tightly connected individuals who bring complementary skills in working through the challenges of the development process. Edison's muckers all knew each other well. They knew Batch had a strong mechanical sense, Boehm was the glass expert, and Upton could tell the story. Together, as an entrepreneurial pocket they leaned heavily on one another's diverse expertise to do rapid development. If a group is too large, it is at risk of losing this level of continuity. Internet giant Amazon recognizes this challenge and therefore employs what it calls the "two pizza rule" to overcome this issue. The "two pizza rule" stipulates that a team shouldn't have more people than two pizzas can feed. Amazon recognizes that the richness of interactions begins to deteriorate as a team's size grows, and that small teams make it easier to communicate and enable people to move quickly with high degrees of autonomy to innovate. Organizational psychologist J. Richard Hackman's research explains the "two pizza rule" more scientifically. He says the challenge isn't the size of the team, but the number of connections that must be nurtured.[9] In a team of 6 individuals, 15 connections must be nurtured for a fully cohesive team. If a group grows to 12, the number increases to 66 connections. Finally, in a group of 50 people, the number of connections increases exponentially to 1,225 ties, making it nearly impossible for everyone to know what everyone else is working on, thus stalling local development. Connectors, however, recognize that development happens best in small, cohesive entrepreneurial pockets. They create development connections, thereby enhancing agility.

Deep Ingenuity of Central Connectors

Many central connectors are also able to acquire a deep expertise within a given domain. This is often the result of a fierce focus on development. They attract people with the same interest and are therefore surrounded by people who share their intense focus. Much of their time is spent refining, enhancing, and perfecting a core area of focus. They are masters on a mission.

Kyle Vogt has this type of focus. Vogt is the co-founder and CEO of Cruise Automation, a driverless car start-up that was acquired by General Motors in 2016. He has had a longstanding obsession with designing a self-driving car. In high school he built a miniature dune buggy that used a webcam to detect lane markings to independently steer within a defined course. He entered his vehicle in the school's science fair and won in a landslide. As a student at MIT he programmed a Ford F-150 to drive itself across the Nevada desert as part of a DARPA Challenge.[10] His dream is to develop a self-driving car that can be safely deployed at scale in the most challenging urban environments.

Cruise operates out of a warehouse-style office in San Francisco's SoMa neighborhood.[11] If you peek behind the curtain, what you'll see looks like many other start-ups, a tight band of twenty- and thirtysomethings in jeans, T-shirts, and hoodies, all with headphones on. But look deeper and what you will notice is an intense group of autonomous engineers, mapping technicians, software engineers, and data scientists all scrutinizing data from automated driving tests and fleshing out the algorithms that lie behind Cruise's self-driving capabilities. The technology uses these algorithms to interpret and manage a complex interplay of sensory inputs associated with road patterns, driving, map routes, lane position, speed, cars, pedestrians, obstacles, and road surface. Self-driving development has become a math challenge, and Vogt's network of friends and colleagues are determined to solve it. Kyle Vogt is the central connector in this network (as represented by one of two center dots in Figure 3.1), and Cruise is a cohesive group of two-pizza teams of developers deeply focused on getting a self-driving car on the road, safely. Through fierce focus and rapid iteration, these teams have been able to progress through four generations of its self-driving technology in just under 18 months. Development connections are facilitating agility.

FIGURE 3.1 Cruise Automation Development Network

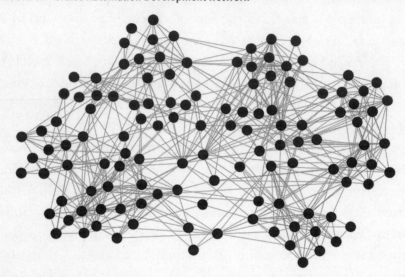

One of the problems when a large corporate giant acquires a start-up is that the synergies that drove the acquisition dissipate quickly. The swift, entrepreneurial nature of the start-up then collides head-on with the operational systems and politics of the slow-moving, risk-averse larger corporation. Soon after, the start-up loses its mojo and the founder's passion begins to feel more like a job. But GM intentionally structured the Cruise deal to minimize this effect. Cruise continues to operate as an independent subsidiary with intentional connectivity to GM. The deal incentivizes critical talent to stick around by hitting technological milestones. The brilliance in this design is seen most clearly, however, within the Adaptive Space that was created. This space enables Cruise to remain densely cohesive with intentional development connections to drive fast progress while building brokerage bridges to the core of GM.

Adaptive Space has therefore enabled Cruise to both move fast and execute with great discipline, while exchanging insights with the core of GM. Doug Parks, GM's vice president for autonomous technology and vehicle execution, describes it as a "give-and-take" model. He says, "They're focused on getting two to three cars to work, and we're focused on getting 20,000 to 30,000 cars to work."[12] This embedded tension enables both groups to quickly discover, develop, and ultimately commercialize a self-driving car at scale.

In this space, Parks is the broker and Vogt is the fiercely focused central connector. Because the core of GM isn't designed to move fast, Adaptive Space helps bridge the differences so GM and Cruise can learn from each other while continuing to leverage what each does best. For example, Parks's team has abandoned the daily staff meeting, where everyone reviews projects, and instead implemented a Cruise-like daily 15-minute blitz to discuss daily challenges that need to be solved. The result has been accelerated decisions within 24 hours. Meanwhile, Cruise gets to enjoy the benefits of GM's experienced engineering expertise and access to testing facilities. Parks and his team act as a bridge to the core engineering team when something needs fixing on one of Cruise's modified Chevy vehicles. Rather than spending hours trying to figure something out, the self-driving start-up team members are able to connect with the parts engineer to resolve it quickly and get back to doing what they do so well— working on the algorithms for self-driving. With Parks serving as the broker, Vogt is able to work exclusively as the central connector, thus keeping his team focused on one thing, "the plan" to get self-driving cars on the road. And as one reporter so aptly noted, "The clock is ticking, and their legacy is on the line."[13]

The Cruise acquisition has positioned GM as a leader on the self-driving vehicle landscape. Within months of the partnership, they had more than 50 self-driving Bolt EVs deployed for testing in San Francisco, Scottsdale, and metro Detroit. Just 18 months after the Cruise deal was announced, GM became the first company to assemble self-driving test vehicles in a mass production facility. GM's president, Dan Ammann, once said, "As the two teams worked closer and closer together, there was this realization that what the other guys did was really difficult."[14] Ammann should know—he was the one who orchestrated the $1 billion acquisition. He has also remained actively engaged to ensure that Cruise remains independent from the core of GM so that it can fiercely focus on the development of self-driving technology, saying, "We are inventing a lot as we go. No one's ever done this before." Ammann knows that this requires development connections and that he needs to protect this investment to ensure a large-scale deployment of self-driving vehicles.

Ammann has also been instrumental to filling in the development gaps. In late 2017 he orchestrated another deal to acquire the lidar technology company Strobe as a missing piece. In an interview with Bloomberg Television on how to build out the technology, Ammann said, "We believe the best way to do that is having all the capability under one roof."[15] He recognizes that to accelerate the development process, a set of tight connections is necessary, later saying, "All of our focus right now is on moving as fast as we can to get to commercial deployment of this technology in the safest way possible." GM seems to be moving faster than its rivals, assembling the in-house capability to engineer, develop, and manufacture self-driving vehicles. The company has indicated that it could start testing a robot taxi service within a few years. Vogt is the fiercely focused central connector in this process while Ammann and Parks are the brokers who have created the Adaptive Space necessary to give GM the inside track for self-driving vehicles. Perhaps Vogt states this best: "By developing the next-generation self-driving platform in San Francisco and manufacturing these cars in Michigan, we are creating the safest and most consistent conditions to bring our cars to the most challenging urban roads that we can find."[16] By creating development connections, GM is doing its best to position itself to positively disrupt.

Fierce focus is essential to development. Every distraction disturbs both the cognitive and collaborative development processes. It is not enough to create tightly connected cohesive teams. They must also be fiercely focused on the plan. Amazon describes this as a single-threaded team. That is, each team has one thing it owns collectively. When team members wake up in the morning, they are fixated on that one thing. Everything else is secondary. For example, a member of the Alexa team is focused on how to make the product better; the team isn't distracted by what's happening in the retail business. Amazon thinks of this much in the same manner as application programming interface (API) development. Its teams focus within the pocket on a set of routines and protocols to develop the product, similar to developing application software. They know that a good API acts as a building block for a broader computer program. The same is true for a single-threaded product team. The concepts come together for broader organizational success.

The result is fast, yet comprehensive development. Each entrepreneurial pocket innovates or fails on its own merits. As they succeed, they generate more possibilities for their concept to grow and be scaled. If they are not successful, new connections are forged and team members move on to another single thread. Amazon has created a vibrant set of development connections that makes the company incredibly agile.

Agility from Social Cohesion

In dynamic times, groups need to rapidly adjust in an improvisational manner. Often they aren't afforded the luxury of stopping and discussing a new course of action—they simply have to react in the moment and anticipate that others will respond accordingly. As teams work together over time and develop trust, they can act quickly in conjunction with one another. Cohesion, trust, and clear expectations form a collective, agile intelligence that emerges through experience.

Consider the example of red fire ants, scientifically known as *Solenopsis invicta*. These irritating little creatures were first introduced into the United States from South America in the 1930s, but now infest 13 southeastern states and are continuing to spread as far west as California and as far north as Virginia, outnumbering their native South American ancestors 10 times. Their success is a result of their ability to respond collectively to challenges. They have an amazing aptitude to adapt, regardless of the threat. If there is a flash flood, they will quickly band together and form a huge raft to float on the water until they reach an object they can climb onto until water levels recede. If there is a drought, they forge tunnels that extend deep into the ground to reach the water table. They are amazingly agile, and they do it through a process of collaboration and interaction enabled by shared signals.

The same type of agility can emerge from human systems through cohesive exchanges. A great example can be found in the swiftness of Navy SEAL (Sea Air and Land) teams. These teams routinely face uncertainty in real-time situations. Missions vary radically, from taking out terrorists, to hostage rescues, to recon assignments. However, when something emerges, the SEALs are prepared. They have rehearsed multiple scenarios many times before deployment during SEAL Qualification Training—a grueling process that concludes with five days of nonstop physical exertion and radical sleep deprivation. The team doesn't let up there. Upon graduation, a team does six-month rotations that include 18 more months of training with a six-month deployment rotation built in. Then, they repeat the process. A SEAL's day is filled with physical training that includes such challenges as soft-sand beach runs, long ocean swims, obstacle course drills, and core skills trainings. However, the real preparation is in the generation of mental toughness and cohesion that enables the SEALs to act as a singular unit. Perhaps this is best characterized by Colonel Ardant du Picq's statement: "Four brave men who do not know each other will not dare attack a lion. Four less brave men, but knowing each other well, sure of their reliability and consequently of mutual aid, will attack resolutely."[17]

Beyond the physical discipline and mental toughness of a SEAL lies the deep bond of cohesive trust. SEALs know they can depend on their teammates. The team will be in position when its members enter a burning building, and when a situation shifts. Cohesion acts as the glue that holds everything else together. It creates a sense of loyalty that extends beyond one's personal safety and sacrifice. Cohesion ensures a commitment that it is always about the mission and not about any one individual. It enables the SEALs to move swiftly and with agility.

Organizations could learn a lot from the SEALs. Companies are under assault, and they need to adapt or die. Yet they stubbornly cling to control and command structures that stifle agility. Organizations need to replace hierarchal control structures with distributed decision making within cohesive teams. They need to focus on social cohesion.

Researcher Alex "Sandy" Pentland, who directs the Human Dynamics Lab within the MIT Media Lab, found in one study that tight, cohesive teams can make decisions 20 percent faster than less cohesive teams. In another study, conducted inside a large financial service company, Pentland's research team studied the social interactions of 90 employees across four teams, inside a large call center, for an entire month.[18] The intent of the study was to discover patterns of activity that usually go unobserved in the call center and evaluate the impact of these social interactions. The data was correlated against critical performance and customer satisfaction data, such as average handle time and number of transferred calls, to analyze relationships between traditional performance indicators and the social interactions that take place. The outcome of this evaluation indicated that group cohesion was strongly correlated to average handle time. More cohesive teams outperformed the less cohesive teams significantly on average handle times. The study also demonstrated that employees with higher cohesion scores tended to have higher initial resolution rates. That is, their ability to solve a customer's request at the first point of contact proved to be better than those employees with lower cohesion rates. Additionally, the employees who had in-person conversations with coworkers throughout the day tended to have comparable customer satisfaction ratings, meaning they did not trade off satisfaction for productivity. Such findings are in direct contrast with the way the call center was designed to operate, in which time spent on the phone was considered the critical indicator of efficiency, therefore limiting the amount of interaction with other employees.

FIGURE 3.2 Social Interactions Among Call Center Teams

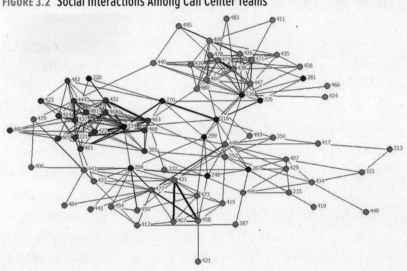

These social interaction patterns are illustrated in Figure 3.2, which visually demonstrates that teams 1 and 3 (the two clusters at the top of the graph) have the highest cohesion scores, while teams 2 and 4 seem to be more loosely connected. Each of these teams is dedicated to very similar work tasks and activities, so the variation of interaction outcomes is independent of responsibilities. The findings have been used to redistribute groups and provide structured team routines to enhance cohesion. Interventions included team huddles, collective breaks, and sharing forums. It turns out that as the teams interacted more with each other and cohesion increased, they became more agile in responding to customers. The impact of these changes was a 25 percent improvement in average handle time, making it clear that cohesion improves agility.

Crafting Development Connections

Brokers introduce ideas, and connectors develop them. Connectors enable Adaptive Space by bringing ideas into reality. They provide the development horsepower to move from concept to breakthrough in much the same manner as Edison's muckers did. Leaders who are facilitating change need to ensure that connectors are engaged when ideas need to be developed and advanced. There are five essential ways to facilitate development connections:

1. **Cultivate entrepreneurial pockets.** Organizations need to forge cohesive relationships within entrepreneurial pockets where ideas can be applied, socialized, tested, and iterated. They need to provide local support to generate a safe and creative environment for experimentation and iteration. They need to drive local application.

2. **Enable central connectors to influence.** Organizations need to ensure that connectors feel supported to fully leverage their central network position. They need to make use of the innate reciprocity and trust of central connectors to facilitate local change. They need to actively engage connectors to get things done.

3. **Protect development pockets.** Organizations need to recognize that development flourishes in small, inner circles of tightly connected individuals. They need to challenge these teams to take bold action and drive rapid development. They then need to step back and protect the boundaries of these pockets so they don't lose continuity in the development process. Principles like the "two pizza rule" are helpful.

4. **Harvest the expertise of central connectors.** Organizations need to fully activate the deep expertise and passion of central connectors. They need to ensure that these individuals are fully devoted to a core domain with limited external distractions. They need to leverage the fierce focus of central experts to attract and challenge others to become "masters on a mission."

5. **Foster social cohesion to drive agility.** Organizations need to focus on generating social cohesion to ensure agility. They need to encourage rapid adjustments and improvisation in response to environmental shifts. They need to cultivate agile intelligence that emerges through experience and cohesion. They need to foster cohesion to create "group flow."

Connectors create development connections that encourage cohesive groups to build out ideas and experiment with agile solutions. The result is ideas are applied, socialized, tested, and iterated on to create bold innovations, positioning an organization to be more agile.

4

•————————•

Diffusion Connections of Energizers

Help young people. Help small guys. Because
small guys will be big. Young people will have
the seeds you bury in their minds, and when
they grow up, they will change the world.

—JACK MA

The documentary *Crocodile in the Yangtze* begins with a Chinese man dressed up in an outlandish rock star outfit that includes a wild wig and lipstick, performing onstage in front of 16,000 people in Yellow Dragon Stadium.[1] As rock concerts go, this might not seem all that strange. However, the man on stage is not a rock star but Alibaba founder and billionaire Jack Ma, speaking at the annual meeting where the people in the audience are the Internet giant's employees. Unsurprisingly, Ma's nickname is "Crazy Jack." Few CEOs act so outrageously in public, but Crazy Jack isn't just any CEO. Ma has built the world's largest e-commerce company, making him the richest man in China and one of the wealthiest men in the world. He is also the kinetic leader who has combined Western and Chinese technologies to challenge global multinational Internet empires such as Amazon and eBay head-on. As the outlandish rock star, Crazy Jack is energizing his employees as he convinces them that "eBay is a shark in the ocean. We are a crocodile in the Yangtze River. If we fight in the ocean, we will lose. But if we fight in the river, we will win."

Perhaps the line between crazy and genius is finer than we think. Alibaba has grown into a powerhouse of three entities: Alibaba International, an online business-to-business market-place; Alibaba China, a Chinese language business-to-business site focusing on domestic trade; and Taobao, an online consumer-to-consumer auction site similar to eBay. The empire also has significant investments in electronic payments, cloud computing, and streaming entertainment. Crazy Jack brilliantly recognized that Alibaba couldn't match the all-star talent of Amazon and eBay, so he had to find ways to energize Alibaba employees to work together. In other words, he had to help ordinary people do extraordinary things. Forget comprehensive data analysis and sophisticated algorithms—Ma and his team had to make decisions based on gut instinct. The Chinese Internet company had to move much more quickly than its competitors. Ma knew that his team had to make mistakes, and that he had to model this if they were to become an action-oriented culture that moved extremely quickly. He knew he had to be outlandish. He needed to open up Adaptive Space, to provide the freedom for employees to take risks. He knew they needed to fail and then follow with rapid adjustments if they were going to be competitive in today's market. To do this, Jack Ma acted as an energizer. Energizers help others to see grander possibilities and encourage them to charge forward in pursuit of these opportunities.

We shouldn't be surprised by Ma's leadership approach. His story is truly a rags-to-riches fairytale.[2] He grew up in Hangzhou, China, during a difficult period when his family had little money. However, he was a determined young boy. Even at a young age, he would ride 40 minutes on his bike every day to an international hotel just so that he could practice speaking English, eventually providing free tours around the city to hone his skills. Mathematics was another thing, however. He failed the national college entrance exam twice by scoring in the lowest percentile in math. Eventually Ma passed and entered what he describes as "Hangzhou's worst college." Upon graduation as an English major, Ma applied to 30 different jobs and was rejected by all of them. He was the only interviewee of 24 candidates who was rejected by KFC. Ma even tried to be a police officer, but was rejected and provided some cruel feedback: "You're no good."

The one thing he was good at was English, so he eventually landed a job teaching the language at a local college, earning $15 a month. Ultimately he started his own translation company, which provided him with the opportunity to travel to the United States, where he was introduced to the Internet, and an idea emerged. What if he could leverage the Internet within China? That dream turned into Alibaba. These early experiences of rejection and failure taught Ma to not take life so seriously, and to be agile. This mindset has generated the world's largest e-commerce company. Jack Ma's personal charm has attracted thousands of business partners and employees to his cause. "Crazy Jack" is a combination of rock star, inspirational sage, and father figure, energizing a tremendously loyal, hardworking group of employees who would charge through walls for him. Ma is also rooting for them, because he knows, based on personal experience, that "small guys will be big."

The Power of Energetic Enthusiasm

Anyone who has spent time within an organization has had the opportunity to experience the energy from the people around him or her. In some cases, there is a noticeable buzz around a team or project in which ideas flow freely and individuals are able to easily build upon the viewpoints of others. Other times, these interactions are simply grueling. We walk away depleted or de-energized. These day-to-day interactions matter significantly. They can act as a catalyst for agility, or they can demoralize people into simply becoming mere passengers on the bus, content to live out the status quo.

For example, in one of our research cases, we studied an organization that had been in a downward business spiral for years. The team had suffered defeat after defeat in the marketplace and was barely clinging to life. Everything they tried seemed to fail. Their fate seemed inevitable, and most people seemed content to simply ride it out. In a final ditch effort to turn things around, management hired a series of high-profile individuals to introduce some new strategies and ideas. One of these individuals was a product-marketing expert who described his first strategy review session as "a welcoming to the land of the living dead." It was as if a dark cloud hung over the team. When he shared an idea, snarky comments were whispered throughout the room. While he had entered excited about the opportunity, he walked away completely demoralized. We have all had these moments when we were de-energized by others. The good news is that this can happen in the positive direction as well, and it doesn't require a whole team to lift us back up.

Network researchers Rob Cross and Wayne Baker conducted a comprehensive study of energy in which they analyzed seven large organizational networks across a financial services firm, a petrochemical business, a government agency, a strategy firm, and three technology companies.[3] They followed up with a series of detailed interviews within each of these firms. Their focus was to more deeply understand the interactions and relationships with people they had identified as either energizing or de-energizing in the networks. What they discovered was amazing: energy—particularly from a person whom they labeled as an "energizer"—has a significant impact on organizational progress. Most leaders spend their time managing performance and information. According to Cross and Baker's research, however, energy outweighs these priorities by a factor of four in driving progress.

Positive energy connections enhance employee performance in terms of productivity, absenteeism, engagement, and job retention within entrepreneurial pockets. However, their impact may be even greater across the broader organization. Baker found that high-achieving organizations, like Alibaba, have three times more positive energizers than average organizations. There are several reasons for this. First, energizers have the distinct ability to actively engage others in progressing an idea forward. That is, they inspire idea diffusion across a network. Second, they enthusiastically encourage others to take action. By the end of a conversation with an energizer, people are compelled to act. Furthermore, not only do energizers have an infectious impact on others, but they also have the ability to inspire more discretionary effort. Finally, energizers attract other people toward an initiative. That is, they attract clusters of people to join in for the cause. Energizers simply open up Adaptive Space for others to prosper. This is the brilliance of "Crazy Jack." He intuitively understood the power of positive energy. He knew that Alibaba didn't have the resources or knowledge to beat eBay, but if he could energize his employees to act as the crocodile in the Yangtze, they could win. Jack Ma acted as an energizer, and he enacted the diffusion connections necessary for Alibaba to succeed by being faster and more agile than eBay.

Presence of Energizers

Energizers like Jack Ma fully engage in their interactions with others, devoting undivided attention in the moment, even to the little guy. They generate energy as a form of social capital that flows in "the space between" individuals. Energizers have a unique ability to spark positive emotions in their day-to-day interactions. They create positive energy. This is the type of energy you get by interacting with someone who makes you feel joyful and energetic. When you are interacting with energizers, you know they care. You know that they are listening and are truly invested in your best interests. They are actively engaged in the moment with you.

Southwest Airlines is known for its high energy and engaging culture. Employees are taught to connect with people and act as champions for the community. They know that whether in the air or on the ground, community is more than a place, it's what brings people together. The company describes this as Southwest Citizenship, in which employees live with a "servant's heart" and "follow the golden rule," treating others with respect. However, at Southwest Airlines these statements extend beyond platitudes. The company's employees embody them. For example, when nine-year-old Gabby Swart was flying Southwest Airlines from Florida to New Jersey, she wasn't feeling very well.[4] Gabby was afraid to fly and when some turbulence hit she suddenly started to panic. Making this situation far more threatening was the fact that she has Type 1 diabetes and her anxiety caused her blood sugar to plummet to potentially dangerous levels. This is when Southwest Airlines fight attendant Jovan "Garrick" Riley stepped in. He noticed the little girl was in distress and calmly asked her mother if she was okay. Gabby's mother didn't quite know how to respond. Garrick, however, gave her a reassuring look and gently asked for permission to assist. He then went into action doing his best to make the young girl laugh. He even brought her a "special drink" to loosen up the tension. It seemed to be working as Gabby began chuckling. Then, when the plane started descending through turbulence, she began crying again. Garrick sat down in the empty seat next to her, and as she grabbed his arm, "He gently told her she could hang on as long as she needed to." After they landed and were taxiing to the gate, Garrick announced on the intercom that his friend, Gabby, in the front row overcame her fears of flying and asked for a round of applause. The whole plane erupted. This is what energizers do. They come alongside, emote positive emotions, and encourage those around them.

Much like Alibaba, Southwest was founded on quirky behaviors. The eccentric airline became the industry's biggest success story by unleashing the energy of employees like Garrick—and therefore, encouraging agility. To understand the peculiar culture of Southwest Airlines, it is important to understand Herb Kelleher. He co-founded Southwest Airlines in 1967 with a revolutionary vision of eliminating unnecessary services and utilizing secondary airports to ensure the lowest fares in the industry. Kelleher was known as a very empathetic and charismatic leader who encouraged his employees to "Be Yourself." When you walk into the company's headquarters, you'll find a gallery of memorabilia in reverence to Southwest's

"Wild Turkey–swilling, Marlboro-smoking co-founder." You'll also find a picture of Kelleher in a sequined Elvis costume and another where he's arm-wrestling an airline rival. Perhaps most illuminating of all is a display where you are able to press a button to hear the former CEO's famous laugh. You have a choice of three versions—"the guffaw, the chortle, and the roaring belly buster."[5] Herb Kelleher was an energizer through and through, even down to his laughs, which seemed to rub off on the Southwest employees like Garrick.

An interaction with an energizer leaves others feeling better. Energizers actively participate in exchanges. You can tell through their body language that they are present. People like Garrick are able to energize others in face-to-face exchanges. These connections are what social scientists call dyadic relationships. A dyad represents two people who are connected to each other. These connections can represent friendships, common interests, or working interactions, and these dyadic relationships are the basic building block for an agile network. They form bonds of social capital that enable the sharing of learning and ideas. As two people extend their connections to others, an informal network emerges. As a result, these interactions become conduits of energy across a broader organization. During face-to-face exchanges emotions are also shared, and depending on the intensity of these emotions, they can have a significant impact on the recipient in the form of energy.

In every face-to-face interaction, individuals transmit unconscious social signals as a complement to their spoken words. Social signals are conveyed in body language, facial expression, and voice inflection. These subtle, nonverbal patterns reveal the individual's belief and attitude toward the other person. This is critical to understanding energizers: they show up differently in interactions—they are fully attentive to the people they are engaging and provide the pace necessary for others to be a meaningful part of the conversation. They have the distinctive ability of demonstrating genuine interest in others and their ideas. During one-on-one interactions, energizers seem to be able to capture the hearts and imaginations of others.

Sandy Pentland at MIT has been studying the impact of social signals for years.[6] His research argues that these signals are not just a complement to our conscious language but form a separate communication network of influencing. He asserts, based in biological development, that social signaling evolved from ancient primate signaling mechanisms and provides an unmatched window to more clearly view intentions, goals, and values. For example, infants learn at an early age to respond to a parent's voice tone or gesture even before they are able to understand language. These early learnings remain in an individual's subconscious brain and prove critical for both determining the effectiveness of face-to-face interactions and the degree of energy emissions. Pentland has suggested that as much as 80 percent of an individual's ability to influence another happens in these face-to-face exchanges.

In one study, Pentland evaluated the face-to-face interactions of a speed-dating event. At the conclusion of the event, participants submit a list of the individuals they would like to share their contact information with to the organizers. There is a match when both parties choose to share contact information with each other. This is fertile territory for studying social signals. Accordingly, Pentland evaluated the social signals in each exchange and then correlated the findings with the actual match decisions, and it turned out that social signals were a significant predictor of a match. By looking only at changes in the consistency of speech patterns and high energy levels, as measured by sensor devices, the team was able to predict with 71 percent accuracy if there would be a match. In short, our social cues have the capacity to forge deep relationships or to convey a level of disinterest that inhibits future interactions.

Understanding how energy is emitted in face-to-face interactions is critical to organizational agility. Positive energy forges trusted relationships. These dyadic relationships become the simple building blocks for agile organizations. They create the critical links for positive energy to readily flow, and these relationships build hope and excitement about new possibilities. Indeed, high-energy dyadic relationships are the foundation of diffusion connections that spread energy and ideas across a network.

Catalyzing Energy in Networks

Energizers tap into existing relationships, spark the interest of others, and unleash the passion necessary for learning, insights, and adaptation. They encourage enthusiasm to drive diffusion, cocreation, and excitement across the larger organization. Energizers challenge people to think more boldly than they would within their entrepreneurial pocket, creating an infectious mindset of progress. They create the potential for new possibilities to emerge by engaging individuals with different expertise or backgrounds in an initiative.

Focusing on possibilities generates energy. These possibilities must be motivating and worthy of people's efforts. Energizers catalyze others to see possibilities, while de-energizers see roadblocks at every turn. We experience this every day; one team member constantly highlights the obstacles to getting something done, while another has the propensity to see opportunities beyond the roadblocks. In one of our research cases, a senior person, within a product development group, was known for highlighting all the reasons why something couldn't be done. He was a self-proclaimed pragmatist and was rarely able to see the broader possibilities on the horizon. Another, more junior person within the group seemed to always have a positive response to overcome the obstacles. She was able to envision more encouraging sets of possibilities. She became a compelling informal leader who energized those around her to develop bolder products, eventually designing, developing, and launching one of the more successful products in the company's history. Seeing grander possibilities matters.

This is what we see with Mary Barra, General Motors' chairman and CEO. Barra has the capacity to see over the horizon and catalyze others toward new possibilities. She has outlined a compelling vision to be part of a world with "zero crashes, zero emissions and zero congestion."[7] Far more important than the vision, however, is the belief she and others have instilled in the company since she took the reins. She and her team have developed a road map that addresses challenges such as crashes, pollution, and congestion in a world of rising urbanization. Barra believes that, "by working together, we can solve these challenges and deliver safer, better and more sustainable transportation solutions for all of our customers."[8] She believes that the future of mobility will be driven by the convergence of electrification, autonomous vehicles, and connectivity and shared mobility services. Most important, she has created the Adaptive Space necessary for others to see greater possibilities. For example, each year she issues a series of grand challenges to 35 different senior executives in which they are to reimagine what's possible in the emerging mobility world. These leaders are organized into multiple cross-functional teams dedicated to more deeply understanding future possibilities. These teams engage in challenges such as reimagining commuter transportation, reimagining mobility for the youth, or reimagining mobility for working mothers, to name a few, and the teams use design thinking to actively engage with customers, cities, and potential partners to uncover new solutions. The result has not only been a set of new bold solutions, but a newfound belief that by working together to explore possibilities, GM can deliver safer, better sustainable transportation solutions.

In this way, Barra has energized the team to think more boldly. Energizers create space for others to engage in challenges. They are driven toward a vision yet they are open and flexible about how to get there. They enable growth to occur in unanticipated ways as people determine, on their own, how to move an idea forward. Energizers have the distinct ability to attract others to an initiative and motivate them to take action. The reputation of an energizer spreads quickly, attracting others to a cause and catalyzing them to engage more confidently than before.

Rob Cross and Wayne Baker studied one large petrochemical organization that had recently launched a culture change initiative to drive engagement and performance. The organization had been struggling. As a result, senior executives recognized the need to bring in some new leaders to inspire change. After bringing in three new leaders from outside the group, they decided to run a network analysis to determine the impact. Figure 4.1 represents this study; the three light circles in the center are the leaders who were brought in to help shift the organizational culture. In analyzing the number of incoming connections, it becomes clear that this strategy had a significant impact. Removing these three energizers from the network would virtually divide the diagram into two major parts and significantly reduce the energy of the group. These energizing ties serve as the lifeblood of an organization and enable its agility.

FIGURE 4.1 Energizing Connections of Leaders

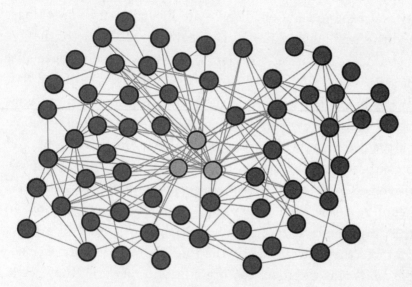

Additionally, it is important to note that trust is essential to creating positive emotions. People are more likely to be energized by someone with a compelling idea who is considered trustworthy, yet they would likely dismiss the very same idea from someone who has a reputation for being untrustworthy. To build this type of trust, energizers consistently follow up what they say with actions, and they reliably follow up on their commitments. They also maintain a balance between what they gain and what they contribute to their network. They build a reputation for driving organizational progress, even above their own self-interest. Finally, energizers ensure that the people they interact with get credit for their efforts. They are quick to publicly recognize and encourage others.

People walk away from energizers feeling more inspired to take action. They are more willing to step forward and take risks. These energizing connections prompt greater creativity and experimentation. People are moved to try new things, and this isn't just social, it's also neurological. "Land of the living dead" experiences, similar to what the product specialist described earlier in this chapter, trigger a threat response that diverts blood flow away from the brain's working memory function, which processes new information and ideas. It puts people on the defensive, which impairs thinking, creative insight, and breakthroughs. Energizers, on the other hand, promote positive emotions in their exchanges, therefore prompting a positive neural response, which opens up creativity and imagination. In this way people acting as energizers have a multiplying effect on those they interact with. The result is that they attract people who want to propel the organization forward. They act as a magnetizing force, pulling people in. This increases organizational interconnectivity around a movement, unleashing the interest of the individuals and promoting change. The effect is idea diffusion. Energizers create idea diffusion connections, which enhance organizational agility.

Contagious Nature of Energizers

The definition of diffusion is the spreading of something more widely. More specifically, in chemistry it is the movement of particles from a high concentration area to lower concentration areas. For example, when a teabag is placed in water, it will diffuse throughout the cup. This process is accelerated when the water is heated and stirred. Energizers help to both heat and stir the water to accelerate diffusion. In much the same manner as a tea bag, an entrepreneurial pocket is heavily concentrated with a few ideas or insights. Energizers create diffusion connections to help spread these ideas to less concentrated areas of the network. In this process, much like the teacup, Adaptive Space provides the boundaries necessary so that this diffusion doesn't become so diluted that its effects are limited.

For years, companies have taught managers how to drive change throughout organizations, spending considerable time developing elaborate blueprints for these efforts, including a compelling vision to pull people forward, a clearly articulated sense of urgency to move people out of the status quo, a well-crafted communication plan so everyone is on the same page, and a comprehensive stakeholder engagement strategy to get buy-in from key stakeholders. More often than not, however, these change efforts fail to reach expectations. In reality, efforts to manipulate our way through the hierarchy are rarely effective at driving significant behavioral change.

Fortunately, our emerging understanding of networks suggests an alternative, or at least a complementary approach. We seem to have a remarkable ability to influence the behavior of those closest to us—that is, of our relationships out to three degrees of separation. In other words, we have the ability to influence our friends' friends' friends. Nicholas Christakis and James Fowler call this the Three Degrees of Influence Rule, which states that our behaviors have the capacity to ripple across our networks, contagiously, within three degrees of separation.[9]

Beyond three degrees, our ability to influence others substantially decreases.

To illustrate this concept, let us consider the example of smoking cessation. Over the past 40 years, the percentage of smoking adults has dropped from 45 to 21 percent. Individuals have been quitting in droves. Consequently, it now appears that while smoking is clearly addictive, quitting is *contagious*! Indeed, Christakis and Fowler studied a densely interconnected social network of 12,067 people from 1971 to 2003 to examine the effects of smoking cessation and found that it occurred at the highest frequency in clusters across the social network. In other words, the decision to quit smoking was not isolated to the individual. Instead the analysis showed discernible clusters of smokers and nonsmokers and that these clusters extended to three degrees of separation. Consequently, despite the decrease in smoking within the overall population, clusters of smokers remained about the same size, suggesting that while networks of three degrees of separation were quitting in concert with one another, other clusters continued smoking, also in concert with one another. Furthermore, it was determined that the behavior of those who were closest to an individual had the greatest impact on smoking cessation. For example, the risk for smoking for a person connected to a smoker at one degree of separation is 61 percent higher, on average, than would be expected as a result of chance. The risk is 29 percent higher at two degrees of separation, that is, when friends of that person's friends smoke. Finally, the risk is 11 percent higher if the friends of the person's friends' friends smoke. Thus, according to this study, individuals have a remarkable ability to influence the behavior of those closest to them, and therefore they can enact local change that can quickly spread across the broader network.

In 2014, General Motors launched a grass roots initiative called GM2020 to open up Adaptive Space so individual employees could connect and create across teams. The auto giant knew that it had to positively disrupt the way that individuals interacted to more boldly unleash its own creative potential from within. It needed to create Adaptive Space to promote the energy of brokers across teams to enhance discovery, then leverage the trust of connectors to energize within their own natural entrepreneurial pockets to spread ideas. The result has been a multitude of adaptive solutions: one group created a new process to improve buyer/supplier relationships; another developed a millennial-friendly interviewing process; another created monthly cross-departmental sessions designed to share problems and proactively identify organizational roadblocks.

The Adaptive Space generated from a GM2020 event could take the form of a Co-Lab, a Summit, a Tipping Forward event, or any number of employee-developed constructs. For example, a Co-Lab is a 24-hour intensive challenge event that is part shark tank and part hackathon. A Co-Lab represents as many as 60 individuals from across various groups competing as small teams to build prototypes and pitch ideas to executive leaders. A GM2020 Adaptive Space activity might also be a large-scale event, such as a 2020 Summit or a Tipping Forward session. A Summit is a catalyst event that includes as many as 500 individuals acting as brokers and connectors from across functions, using design-thinking methods to share, create, and build solutions. A Tipping Forward event usually includes 300 to 600 individuals and creates Adaptive Space by allowing people to openly share the many successes that have been applied locally and to then tap into the passion of energizers to amplify these successes across the broader enterprise. In the spirit of Adaptive

Space, GM2020 encourages individuals to leverage their own networks to create their own solutions. A 2016 *Fast Company* article entitled "GM to Top Tech Talent: Ditch Silicon Valley for Detroit" described GM2020 as a "culture club" of activities.[10] For example, a small group of engineers and researchers launched an internal Maker Space to encourage cross-group tinkering to build early prototypes of vehicle features. An internal learning community held a Learn Con event to unleash more creativity across functions, while yet another group launched internal TEC (technology engineering and creativity) Talks, designed to feature monthly presentations from internal experts. At the end of the day, GM2020 created Adaptive Space to spark the movement of ideas and information across the organization.

At the center of the GM2020 community network are Laurie Asava and Rachel Rosenbaum, both of whom have played an essential role in crafting solutions and enabling deployment. They have also been energizers. GM2020 has been catapulted across southeast Michigan because Asava and Rosenbaum buzzed up the network. Asava helped to launch GM2020 in 2014 and has been central in energizing a base of volunteers who continue to positively disrupt the organization. Rosenbaum, on the other hand, has attracted employees to engage in an assortment of design thinking activities that place the customer's needs in the center of improvements. For example, she drove a major initiative to "reimagine the way rising female talent gains access to senior leaders." Together, the duo has energized others to self-organize into small local and cross-functional groups to solve problems ranging from workplace concerns to interior vehicle design and innovation processes. Figure 4.2 illustrates the energizing effect the duo has had on a network of over 700 volunteers. Asava and Rosenbaum are represented by the two larger dots in the center of the network diagram. The connections that emanate from the two, visualized in the denser, darker portion of the network, represent the energy they exhibit across the network.

FIGURE 4.2 **GM2020 Energy Network**

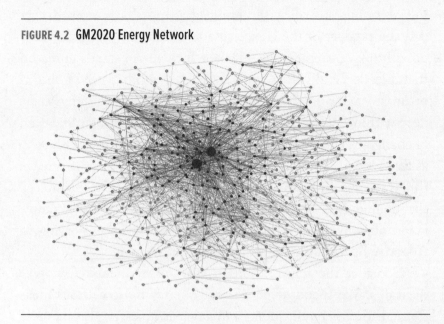

Together, the duo represents nearly 23 percent of the energizing ties in the network. This energy has spread to others in the same manner as Christakis and Fowler's research would have predicted. Indeed, the movement is predicated on this premise. During many of these events, people can be seen wearing a blue 2020 T-shirt and acting out high-energy skits to illustrate various experiences. These lighthearted theatrical skits bring a variety of serious workplace issues out in the open so that people move beyond whining and are encouraged to go do something. The enthusiasm is contagious, and Asava and Rosenbaum have been essential in energizing this movement.

As GM2020 demonstrates, the contagious nature of our interactions shifts energy patterns in a remarkable manner. As energy spreads across the network, it results in coordinated actions. Accordingly, it appears that altering a behavior, such as smoking cessation, isn't solely the result of a leader's decision. Rather it is the product of the choices made within a cluster of friends or within an entrepreneurial pocket. It therefore stands to reason that if leaders really desire to activate change, they need to begin by understanding network dynamics. Indeed, a few individuals, deep within a network, have the potential to create a groundswell of change by simply energizing others to act upon their beliefs—as we saw with GM2020. This notion radically shifts the way we think about agility, leading us to consider the strong possibility that change isn't really organizational at all but rather a compilation of individuals' behaviors. That is, a few friends acting in Adaptive Space can generate a contagious movement.

Consider the ramifications of this phenomenon for organizations. We spend much of our time trying to sell our ideas through the hierarchy, doing whatever it takes to get the most senior people available to buy into our concept, thinking that if they become advocates, we will be successful. Unfortunately, this strategy rarely works. At best we get lukewarm buy-in, and when these ideas are challenged, senior leaders easily waver. Ideas are far more likely to garner attention and build momentum when they are first shared in one's natural clusters, leading to the question: "What if our energy were focused on selling our ideas into local entrepreneurial pockets?" Christakis and Fowler's research illustrates that an individual's energy can shift that of a local cluster or entrepreneurial pocket, and therefore create a groundswell. Furthermore, their study suggests that people are more directly influenced by their local relationships than they are by top-down visions. In other words, if you want to spread something fast, tap into the natural human networks, or the entrepreneurial pockets of activity that surround you, first rather than taking it to your boss. This is what Asava and Rosenbaum did.

Crafting Diffusion Connections

Brokers introduce ideas, connectors develop them, but energizers spread them. Energizers trigger the interest of others and unleash the passion necessary for bold solutions to advance. Network energy drives diffusion, cocreation, and active engagement across the larger organization. It challenges people to think more boldly than they can within their own subgroups, creating a contagious mindset that amplifies ideas. Energizers have the distinct ability to attract others to an initiative and inspire them to take action. They are able to fully engage in interactions, motivating others to devote more time and energy to an initiative.

An energizer is able to build a reputation for providing support to others that spreads quickly across the network. Energizers tend to get the most out of others, and they are more likely to get ideas noticed and ultimately aggregated into bolder, integrated concepts. It is therefore critical for an organization to capitalize on its energizers. There are four essential ways to enable energizers to facilitate diffusion connections in an organization:

1. **Provide space for energizers to engage.** Energizers create positive energy through their ability to empathize.

Organizations need to fully leverage this capability by providing intentional space for energizers to actively listen to others. They need to emphasize the importance of these interactions in the same manner Southwest Airlines does. They need to encourage energizers to be fully attentive and provide the space for others to be meaningful parts of the conversation.

2. **Focus on bold possibilities.** Energizers challenge people to think more boldly. Organizations need to leverage energizers to catalyze others toward grander possibilities. They need to drive toward a vision yet provide the flexibility for others to engage in moving an idea forward. They need to leverage the reputation of an energizer to attract others to a cause.

3. **Focus on generating energizing ties.** Energizing connections serve as the lifeblood of an organization and enable agility. Organizations need to recognize that trust is essential in generating positive emotions. They need to nurture this type of trust and reinforce the need to follow up on commitments. They need to inspire others to take action and to ensure that people are encouraged and publicly recognized for their contributions.

4. **Encourage diffusion beyond pockets.** Energizers create diffusion connections, enhancing organizational agility. Organizations need to actively facilitate the spreading of ideas beyond current entrepreneurial pockets. They need to diffuse these ideas to less concentrated areas of the network as well as to create Adaptive Space so that the diffusion doesn't become too diluted. They need to tap into the contagious nature of interactions to carry energy and ideas.

Energizers create the diffusion connections that leverage the contagious nature of face-to-face relationships. The result is that ideas flow freely and individuals are able to easily build upon the viewpoints of others—positioning an organization toward increased agility.

5

●────────────────●

Disruptive Connections of Challengers

*I believe you have to be willing to be
misunderstood if you're going to innovate.*

—JEFF BEZOS

E ver since it was founded in 1994, the titanic online empire
Amazon has had inimitable ambitions. The company began
as an online bookstore, recognizing that brick-and-mortar
retail stores could offer only up to 200,000 different titles, but
an online bookstore could offer significantly more at less cost.
Of course, to do so, the company would have to have whole-
sale access to books, centralized distribution centers, and a
strong logistics network. Jeff Bezos, the company's founder,
has always challenged conventional wisdom. If Bezos is nothing else, he is persistent. He even considered naming his online
store Relentless, purchasing the URL Relentless.com.[1] Friends
convinced him that the name sounded a bit sinister. So Bezos
instead selected Amazon because the Amazon is a place that is

exotic and different, just as he envisioned his company would be. The Amazon is also the biggest river in the world, measured by water volume, and that represented just how large his ambitions were for his company.

From the time Bezos began Amazon, he was relentless in insisting that the customer is king and the company would focus on a long-view perspective. For years, investors criticized Amazon for continually not living by the rules of profitability. Many serious investors argued that Amazon was fundamentally flawed as a business model and the company would never make money. Bezos's response was to ignore the critics, and to challenge Amazon to focus on growing revenues. Even from the beginning, the company's business plan was unusual. Bezos did not expect to make a profit during the first five years. Amazon instead focused on growth, expanding one business sector after another, providing customers with superior service. Bezos then challenged conventional wisdom again by taking profits from one line of business and investing them into a new one, fueling an expansion model, and almost completely ignoring the investor community. As Bezos once said, "I believe you have to be willing to be misunderstood if you're going to innovate." Accordingly, he hasn't exactly concerned himself with being misunderstood. He has simply remained fierce about offering consumers the lowest possible prices in order to build loyalty and grow the business.

Perhaps Amazon's true brilliance is found in its ability to persistently experiment and usher in new ideas. The company employs an excellent example of the Adaptive Space approach to innovation. Local entrepreneurial pockets experiment with ideas and then connect with others to get those concepts scaled into the broader platform. The founder kindles this mindset. Bezos credits the summers he spent fixing windmills and repairing equipment on his grandparents' ranch in Texas with shaping his zeal toward experimentation.[2] He spent his long summer days tinkering with equipment and experimenting with whatever resources were around, and he was relentless in making things better. This is the same approach Amazon employs today. Bezos once proclaimed, "I think frugality drives innovation, just like other constraints do. One of the only ways to get out of a tight box is to invent your way out."[3] His persistence to challenge others in making things better and pushing the boundaries of what's possible has propelled Amazon to be the world's largest and most successful Internet retail company. Originally both exotic and different, it truly has become much like the largest river in the world.

Jeff Bezos is a challenger. He is able to see new opportunities where others don't. He is also willing to disrupt the current order of things and push toward those overlooked possibilities. Challengers also tend to be pragmatic visionaries. That is, they can see the future more clearly than most, and are disciplined in moving toward it. They are willing to experiment and iterate forward, challenging those around them to explore new possibilities. Like Bezos, many of the best challengers are relentless in this pursuit.

Brokers discover ideas, connectors develop them, and energizers diffuse them. Challengers, on the other hand, provoke positive disruption to usher in new ideas as the new normal. They ignite change from within an organization by leveraging external pressures as catalysts for change. They enable agility by positively disrupting the status quo and breaking down barriers to progress. Old habits are hard to break. Challengers recognize that the world is changing rapidly and they need to position their organizations to respond wisely to these changes. The advantage still goes to the initial disruptor. There is a caveat to this, however: it is always easier to be the disruptor when you aren't disrupting yourself. Challengers know this and therefore take a long view of success, while acknowledging that short-term distress is almost always inevitable.

Within conventional organizations, operating structures have been designed to focus on short-term performance. The result is that many formal leaders act as roadblocks to new ideas and innovations. They are responsible for resource optimization and daily outcomes. New ideas, especially the bolder ones, provide no short-term benefits. In fact, these ideas frequently add risk and variation, the very things the operating system has been designed to reduce. This creates a natural propensity for leaders to be conservative. Consider the research case shown in Figure 5.1, where individuals within the network were asked with whom they were most reluctant to share their ideas. The results showed that people, in general, were most reluctant to share their ideas with their leaders (leaders are represented by the white dots in the center of the diagram). This is typical in many organizations; leaders are so focused on short-term performance that they often view ideas that enhance longer-term benefits as noise. Therefore they are often inclined to dismiss them, suggesting that "we need to stay focused on our priorities."

This phenomenon shows why challengers are so critical to organizations. They recognize the natural propensity of organizations to shut down ideas, and they find ways to circumvent the stifling effect. Challengers like Bezos are incredible at taking a long-term approach and provoking positive disruption. They are able to tap into network buzz to ensure that ideas are openly shared and more fully developed into breakthrough concepts for the future. Challengers create the connections necessary to disrupt existing structures and allow the active flow of new ideas. They positively disrupt.

FIGURE 5.1 Sharing Reluctance Network

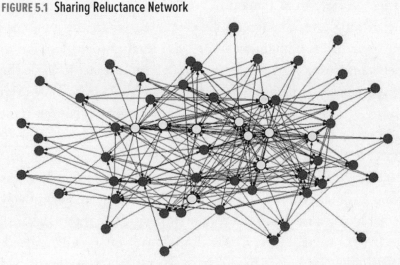

Connecting for Positive Disruption

Positive disruptions are not always enabled from the top down. Sometimes they evolve from a set of emergent responses. Just consider the Egyptian revolution. On January 25, 2011, tens of thousands of protesters, fed up with high levels of poverty, corruption, and unemployment, gathered in the streets of major Egyptian cities for what they called a "Day of Revolt," and demanded change. In the days that followed, millions of protesters gathered in Cairo's Tahrir Square and insisted their dictatorial president, Hosni Mubarak, be removed from office.

After two weeks of unwavering protest, Mubarak resigned from office, on February 11, ending his 30-year reign.

Interestingly, the relatively peaceful revolution did not seem to have a clear leader. Instead, young Egyptians, who were members of a hyperconnected generation, guided the revolt through social media, while remaining mostly anonymous because of their strong fear of a secret police counterattack.[4] These protesters nevertheless brought an impressive level of sophistication to their cause, exploiting the anonymity of the Internet to elude the secret police and planting false rumors to fool spies. They even staged "field tests" in the slums of Cairo before laying out their final battle plans, which included a periodic protest schedule to conserve their energies and resources. In short, the young protestors created Adaptive Space to design a revolution that was exceedingly agile, allowing them to move swiftly and effectively iterate in response to the Egyptian authorities' countermeasures.

In a connected society, behaviors spread very rapidly. Indeed, it was only days before the "Day of Revolt" that Egyptians had watched a Tunisian uprising that led to the resignation of long-time president Zine El Abidine Ben Ali. By witnessing these events unfold through YouTube videos, Facebook posts, and tweets, the young Egyptians were emboldened to start a revolt of their own. Armed with laptops and a courageous vision of freedom, the Egyptian masses thus succeeded in bringing about a peaceful revolution and overthrowing their dictator. The young Egyptians created disruption connections to build momentum and enable Adaptive Space wherever possible in the face of an oppressive regime. They acted as challengers and positively disrupted an entrenched government.

These same connections can be used to enable organizational agility within corporations. IBM has fundamentally reinvented itself multiple times. The company first grew to prominence with punch card machines. Then, in 1953, IBM developed the first commercially successful general-purpose computer. Its inventor, Thomas Johnson Watson Jr., a challenger, had to convince the company's CEO, his father, Thomas Johnson Watson Sr., that the new computer would not harm IBM's profitable punch card business in the immediate future.[5] As a result, the general-purpose computer was designed to circumvent this concern by being incompatible with punch card processing equipment. IBM was trying to prolong the existence of the punch card processing revenue and at the same time build its disruptor—proactively thinking about the decline of the life cycle for one business while also considering the creation of its replacement business. It was a move that fundamentally changed the way the company thought about positive disruption. In fact, IBM has systematically ushered in positive disruptions and phased out current less lucrative or declining businesses ever since. The company has astutely reinvented itself from within.

IBM dominated the mainframe computing industry for years, but it became interested in the personal computer market in the late 1970s after watching Apple and Atari enter the scene. William Lowe, director of IBM's Boca Raton Labs, took a proposal to the management committee in 1980, suggesting they acquire Atari. His proposal was rejected. Instead, Lowe was directed to personally bring an IBM designed product to market within a year.[6] The project was codenamed Project Chess. Lowe conscripted 12 of the company's best engineers into a development team called the "dirty dozen" to work on the project. They were tasked with creating a new computer quickly and preempting competitive products from becoming the de facto standard. In less than a month, the team had already built a prototype personal computer. When Project Chess was completed, the "dirty dozen" had developed a PC that was smaller, cheaper, and easier to use than competitive products. The rest of the story is history.

Since then, IBM's innovations in software, memory, data-bases, and, most recently, cognitive computing have each led to additional billion-dollar businesses. It seems that each time IBM entered into a new era, it responded with new solutions. The company has become tremendously agile. For decades it has dominated the research landscape, scouting for discoveries. However, IBM propels far beyond unearthing new insights by consistently designing useful solutions and facilitating development connections in the same manner as Project Chess. Then the company positions these new products to be operationally scaled. For example, the PC business was headquartered in Boca Raton so that it couldn't be cannibalized by the much more entrenched mainframe business. By partitioning it off, the PC business didn't have to compete for support resources. Finally, as previously mentioned, IBM systematically disrupts existing businesses in order to usher in the new ones. For example, IBM sold the anchor of its laptop business, the ThinkPad, to Lenovo. IBM wanted to get out of the hardware business to focus on cognitive computing and services. Enter Watson, the latest of IBM's agile moves.

It might appear that the disruption connections of the Egyptian revolution and IBM's continual reinvention are extreme cases compared to most organizations. In one situation a groundswell of Adaptive Space was unleashed and a dictator was forced to concede his position, while in the other case, executive leaders recognized the need for change and formally challenged the "dirty dozen" to usher in a new possibility. For organizations to be agile, a little of both is necessary. They must create Adaptive Space so disruption can emerge when needed, and they must formally challenge the organization to be bolder. However, positive disruption is only the beginning. For disruption to take hold, a new normal must also be established.

Facilitating Creative Destruction

Agility requires that leaders create Adaptive Space for dissent to emerge. They also, at times, need to formally commission bold new initiatives that challenge the status quo. However, neither of these strategies is particularly effective without some willingness to acknowledge the potential destruction to the current core business. That is, dissent can't manifest into a movement under the stifling power of a rigid operational system. In fact, even sponsored initiatives risk being strangled out by the dominance of a current business success.

Consider the Motorola cell phone. The company dominated the industry in the late 1990s. Everyone in the United States wanted a Motorola analog phone. However, at the same time, the company had entrepreneurial pockets of network engineers who were investing aggressively in the early development of digital technology for mobile phones. In fact, Motorola not only owned many of the critical patents for the emerging digital platforms, but also was keenly aware of the digital network ascent in Europe and Asia as it was yielding lucrative streams of royalties from these patents. Nevertheless, Motorola's chief executives, blinded by their current success, were unable to see the importance of the digital emergence looming on the horizon

Even more ironic, however, was the fact that while Motorola was engaged in a bloody battle against its chief competitor,

Qualcomm, hundreds of Motorola's network engineers were walking around with Qualcomm digital phones. As the company's former controller, Mike DiNanno, once said, perhaps melodramatically, "There was not a Motorola phone anywhere in the building."[7] Amazingly, the looming disaster could not get the attention of senior executives. The network engineers were just one small voice in the wilderness, and no one could hear them. After all, the cellular business was still rapidly growing, and Motorola was climbing up the Fortune 500 list and delivering record profits. Accordingly, when the disaster hit, it hit hard. The company fell off a cliff, ushering in Nokia's dominance for the next decade and a half. Motorola was unable to facilitate the disruptive connections internally to make the leap to a digital platform.

Harvard economist Joseph Schumpeter popularized the concept of creative destruction back in 1942.[8] His argument was that surges of innovation would devastate incumbent firms and generate the impetus for new ones to emerge. Even back then, in a relatively stable environment, Schumpeter believed that entrepreneurs fueled the economy by generating growth. The result, he hypothesized, was both successes and failures. That is, new businesses emerge, and incumbent businesses are pressured to adapt or die. Today, creative destruction has become the norm. Schumpeter saw creative destruction as an essential element of macroeconomic progress. In his book *Capitalism, Socialism and Democracy*, Schumpeter wrote:

> *The fundamental impulse that sets and keeps the capitalist engine in motion comes from the new consumers' goods, the new methods of production or transportation, the new markets, the new forms of industrial organization that capitalist enterprise creates.*[9]

Schumpeter recognized that entrepreneurs were the foundation of progress. He saw "creative destruction" as a process in which new technologies and innovations render existing ones obsolete, therefore pressuring existing businesses to adapt or fail. He illustrated this by evaluating the boom in the early nineteenth century that was ignited by the rise of textiles, iron, coal, and steam engines, innovations that were ushered in by the advances in steel production and railroad transportation. He believed that the railroad was a powerful transforming shift in the economy, opening up opportunities while clearing out obsolete technologies like water canals. As railroads extended across the United States, freight charges dropped significantly. However, twentieth-century automobile advancements then eroded the advancements of railroads. Indeed, Schumpeter argued that these booms each "contain seeds of their own destruction."[10]

Schumpeter's argument doesn't just hold true for economies. It happens inside large organizations as well. Stanford professor Charles O'Reilly calls this dynamic the "success syndrome."[11] He suggests that as an organization becomes more successful over time, it builds a set of organizational structures, procedures, and processes to replicate its success. Unfortunately, structural inertia eventually sets in, stifling anything that threatens short-term effectiveness. As a formal operational system is constructed, rigid walls are forged to reinforce expectations and social controls that inhibit innovative behavior, or create organizational lock-in. At this point, the seeds for future destruction have been sown. Much as in the Motorola experience, top executives get locked in the status quo and then are unable to facilitate the connections necessary to navigate the creative destruction of previous successes.

It seems that for many leaders, their response to external threats is reminiscent of the instinctual behaviors of the gorilla.

As the dominant leader, the alpha male silverback is central to making decisions, mediating conflict, and determining the actions of the troop. In short, he maintains control. When challenged by another gorilla, the silverback instinctively responds by aggressively beating his chest, baring his teeth, screaming, breaking branches, and charging to demonstrate his superiority. Confrontation by an outside intruder elicits the same response. In an effort to appear fiercer, the silverback organizes the troop into a large huddle, creating the appearance of being a more formidable opponent. Such behaviors serve the troop well when confronted by a natural predator, but when confronted by new intruders, namely poachers, they have a reverse effect, making them even more vulnerable.

Organizations have likewise become locked in to their own instinctual behaviors in an effort to maintain stability. The problem is that, in a dynamic world, new challenges surface without warning. Therefore, to be successful, organizations must reject the instinctual nature of gorilla management and avoid the trap of becoming locked in to conventional practices, or they too risk extinction.

Challengers are critical to defending against these effects. They confront conventional thinking and methods to inspire a long view of future growth. They are keenly attuned to potentially disruptive external pressures and technological advances. As a result, challengers are able to elucidate these forces to others and push others toward new possibilities well before they are obvious to the organization. To do so, they reach beyond the day-to-day requirements of the insular organization to gain new insights and spur others toward different, more adaptive actions.

This is what is happening with electric vehicles at General Motors. Mark Reuss, GM product chief, is "a V-8 Corvette kind of guy"—a trailblazer who "relishes the fast lane." He spends his Friday afternoons blazing the test track in what are known as "knothole rides," comparing GM products to rival vehicles. As a kid, he and his father would go to the Indianapolis 500 each year. He would get a thrill watching the horsepower race down the straightaway. As Reuss recalls, "the hair on the back of your neck stands up, and I was hooked—big time."[12] However, today, the product chief is engaged in a different kind of race, a race for a "zero emissions future." Reuss and his development group are reinventing the organization. They are shifting from gas-guzzling combustible engines to an all-electric business.

Reuss continues to be a trailblazer, recently declaring a company shift to all-electric vehicles as part of a broader vision of a world with "zero crashes, zero emissions and zero congestion." This all starts with the Chevrolet Bolt EV, the first electric car that cracked the code between long range and affordability. Reuss views the Bolt EV as a platform that provides a window into the future. It is an electric vehicle that unleashes new possibilities from self-driving technology to car sharing. It is also the start of a journey to an all-electric future. Reuss and GM have committed to adding more than 20 new zero emission vehicles to global markets in the next few years. As a challenger, Reuss is carving this path forward through a two-pronged approach to electrification that includes both battery electric and hydrogen fuel cell vehicles. It is a new kind of knothole ride that has huge ramifications for a company and an emissions-free world. Much as IBM did with its mainframe computers, Reuss is forging the connections necessary to usher in all-electric vehicles for the longer term while also ensuring the core business continues to produce in the immediate future—therefore, facilitating creative destruction.

One of the disruptive connections he has forged is with Pam Fletcher, the company's chief engineer for Electrified Vehicles and New Technologies. Fletcher is a bit of a gearhead herself, growing up helping her dad work on the cars he raced on weekends.[13] Later, she spent time developing high-performance engine technology for the late Dale Earnhardt's NASCAR team. More recently, she led the development and launch of the Chevy Bolt. Reuss and the rest of the GM leadership team challenged Fletcher and her team: in late spring of 2013, they were given a year and a half to have a prototype ready. They were also challenged to produce a vehicle that had a charge of 200 miles or more. Fletcher used Adaptive Space to keep a sizable group of talented people on the same path. It worked; the car was selected as the 2017 Motor Trend Car of the Year, and it has also become the primary platform for a zero emissions future.

Encouraging Constructive Dissent

Within most organizations the operational systems drive conformity, immobilizing organizations confronted by new threats, forcing individuals to double down on existing practices when agile responses are most needed. This is why challengers are so crucial to agility. Challengers stir debate to encourage idea refinement and advancement in the face of authority. They know the world is dynamic and what works today will be obsolete tomorrow. They embrace dissent as a necessary element of progress. Dissent is essential to Adaptive Space. Dissent moderates the network's buzz generated by energizers and grounds it in actionable, pragmatic realities. The tension created by challengers ensures ideas and solutions have organizational fitness and can be scaled for greater value. This tension is essential to confront the power of the operational systems, which encourages obedience.

In October of 1973, Israel was surprised by an invasion of a coalition of Arab states led by Egypt and Syria. The event is considered a classic intelligence failure in Israeli history, and it occurred because the military was locked in to a worldview that did not contemplate the possibility of an all-out assault. The signals for the event were there, but obedience discouraged dissent. In response to the event, Israeli Defense Forces created a new role, that of the tenth man. The tenth man principle is simple: appoint someone who will challenge conventional wisdom. Those selected are provided the independence to analyze and actively reconsider the status quo. The tenth man searches for information and arguments that contradict an existing intelligence plan. This person also acts as a sounding board for lower-level analysts who raise issues that might not otherwise be considered by the chain of command.

Agile organizations may not have a tenth man, but they have tolerated dissent for years. For example, 3M's former CEO, William McKnight, once told a young employee to abandon a project he was working on, contending it wasn't worth the investment. The employee, Richard Drew, disregarded his advice and continued to work on the project. The result was the invention of masking tape, one of 3M's central products.[14] At HP, David Packard himself told a young engineer, Chuck House, to abandon a display monitor he was working on. Instead, House started sharing his prototype with customers. The feedback was so positive that he was able to convince his R&D manager to put the monitor into production. The product was a market success, and years later, David Packard presented House with a medal for "extraordinary contempt and defiance." Indeed, it appears endorsing some level of constructive dissent is essential for a company's agility.

The response of McKnight and Packard is certainly not the norm for leaders in most organizations. This level of disobedience is rarely tolerated. In fact, many operational systems and processes have been created specifically to prohibit this type of behavior, and traditional human capital systems systematically remove dissenters from the organization. Just consider such systems as traditional performance management and talent management. They are designed around critical competencies of acceptable behaviors; usually these are grounded in operational system thinking. These systems encourage conformity, and misbehavior leads to retribution.

Interestingly, conformity might be even more prevalent in the informal social groups throughout an organization. For years, social psychologists have been studying the effects of what they call social identity theory, which suggests that the groups people belong to are an important source of self-esteem, creating a sense of belonging. Social psychologists describe this sense of belonging as being part of the "in-group." For example, we are Democrats or Republicans. We are New York Yankees fans or Boston Red Sox fans. Or we are engineers or salespeople. Each of these in-group declarations comes with a set of expectations. Norms and beliefs have been formed over time, and once individuals join the in-group, the presumption is they live within these expectation boundaries and the group becomes the unit of social control.

In-group declarations also divide people into "us" and "them." That is, being in-group separates us from those who are not. Just consider the social experiment used as an advertisement for Carlsberg beer. In the experiment, innocent couples arrive at a *Planet of the Apes* movie in Brussels, Belgium, and are given the last seats available. When the unsuspecting couples enter the 150-seat theater, they discover that the two remaining seats are smack-dab in the middle of 148 intimidating bikers who are glaring down at them, leaving the couple with a painful choice. Do they shuffle past the bikers and squeeze into the final two seats, or do they leave the theater? In the commercial, most couples turn around and leave. However a few brave couples decide to trek their way through the bikers to find their seats. Once they finally sit down, they are rewarded with an ovation of cheering bikers and the uncapping of a couple of Carlsberg beers. It is a hilarious advertisement that rewards the adventurous couples.

While the Carlsberg advertisement exaggerates an in-group extreme with 148 intimidating bikers, the type of fear experienced by the unsuspecting couples happens inside firms every day. However, inside organizations, traversing the "us" and "them" divide is rarely celebrated. Instead, the boundaries created between groups buffers the flow of ideas, insights, and learning throughout an organization, with leaders being perhaps the most buffered of all.

Social psychologist Michael Hogg describes this effect as the "social identity theory of leadership."[15] Hogg suggests that leadership within organizations is a group process that is generated by in-group norming. That means leaders form their own in-group and therefore set behavioral expectations for one another. Prototypical leaders, those with the ideal set of behaviors, emerge as a result of this process and are therefore perceived as being very effective within the leader in-group. In contrast, leaders who deviate from the prototypical norms can be perceived as ineffective, even if they are appropriately responding to external circumstances. This phenomenon of favoring traditional norms over what could be bolder, more agile responses dampens leadership creativity. Furthermore, these norms form a sort of social bubble that limits leadership behaviors and insulates leaders from outside influences and information. This is why challengers are so critical: they have the propensity to act as the "tenth man" actively searching for information that contradicts tradition. Like Jeff Bezos, they are willing to be misunderstood in order to innovate, and they are willing to constructively dissent.

Penetrating the Social Bubble

For ideas and innovations to be useful in driving agility, they need to be formally endorsed. They need to move through the brick wall of the formal operational system to become the new normal. It is only then that these ideas can be scaled for optimal impact. The problem is, in many organizations, those in charge of setting new strategies and policy are often isolated from the rest of the organization. Just consider former Lehman Brothers CEO Richard Fuld's daily commute.[16] He had a limo drive him to a helicopter that flew him to Manhattan, where another limo carried him to the company's building. He could then bypass the employee entrance with direct access to the executive floor. Fuld could literally get to and from his office without encountering a single employee. As a result, Fuld was isolated from the day-to-day activities deep inside the organization and therefore unaware of the emerging challenges.

The greatest obligation of senior leaders is to position a company for success. To do so, they must be keenly aware of what is happening around them. Yet positional power and social identity often insulate them from what is actually going on. Either people elevate them to such esteem that they don't feel comfortable openly sharing, or people are so threatened that they couldn't possibly imagine sharing what they know. For many reasons, the most senior leaders find themselves living inside of a social bubble, cut off from the reality of others' experiences. There is even a television show, *Undercover Boss*, that exploits this notion. A senior executive works undercover to better understand how the organization's employees really work.

Social scientists have found that when faced with a decision about who to listen to, leaders within a cohesive group rely most heavily on their everyday connections. They tend to trust people they know best. The problem is that the redundant connections, residing inside of a highly cohesive social bubble, rarely offer new information. Everyday connections are likely to have similar views, perspectives, and interpretations. The result is even greater isolation. Perhaps one of the greatest examples of this phenomenon is Kodak's invention of the digital camera. In 1975, Steve Sasson, a Kodak engineer, invented the world's first digital camera. The prototype was crude, weighing eight pounds and only able to record 0.01 megapixels in black and white, but it worked!

In his recount of the organization's response, Sasson said that when he presented his invention to the management team, their response was, "that's cute."[17] We shouldn't be surprised by this response; after all, Kodak was a film company, and this is what the team talked about every day. In fact, the company had a commanding 90 percent of the photographic film sales at that time. The management team couldn't be bothered by something so seemingly trivial. It is important to note, however, that Sasson's own team had a very different response. As he put it, "the technical people loved it." After all, they lived in a different bubble, one that served as an entrepreneurial pocket for future innovations. Sadly, the rest of the story is history. The technology was rejected, and Kodak soon after found itself unprepared for the looming disruptions of the digital age, which ultimately led to the company's demise.

A more effective strategy for Sasson would have been to find others that could have helped him penetrate the social bubble. If he had focused more on getting people across the organization, outside of his own entrepreneurial pocket, to talk about his invention instead of trying to sell it himself based on its merit alone, he might have been more successful. Outsiders who are trying to convince someone inside the bubble have two major disadvantages. First, they need to create a compelling case for their idea, and then they need to convince the insiders that they are worth listening to. Either one of these obstacles is daunting; together they can doom an idea for failure. Unfortunately, ideas cannot be separated from those who advocate for them. If Sasson could have gotten others to start talking about his invention, he could have closed the network in on leaders, and he might have created a different outcome. Just consider for a moment, how many times have you heard someone present an idea, only to have it rejected? Then, moments later, a bubble dweller repeats the same idea with a slight twist, and the response is eureka! The only thing that has been significantly changed is the credibility of the presenter.

If people close to the social bubble had been excited about Sasson's invention, they would have echoed it to those closest to them. The novelty would have been shared with an insider or two, closing the network and penetrating the social bubble. Then, when Sasson got his chance, his odds of influencing others would have increased significantly. While it is difficult for outsiders to influence those inside the bubble, they can create an echo that serves to increase acceptance among others. Accordingly, great challengers know how to seed the network by sharing their ideas with critical energizers who echo them throughout the network. This is exactly what we saw in one case where a product designer was attempting to get his new digital feature endorsed by the product review board. Rather than pitching the idea in a conventional manner to the board, he seeded it into his network by sharing a crude prototype with a few energizers. Not only did they like the idea, but they also helped him to enhance it. The result was they echoed the idea across the network. Eventually the review board heard about the idea from within their own social bubble, and the designer was asked to share it as part of a formal review. This is called network closure. Figure 5.2 shows the effects of this seeding across the network. The small isolated cluster on the far right represents the review board, and the product designer is the small white dot in the center. He was able to share his idea with a few critical contacts (represented by the grey nodes), and they echoed it into the social bubble of the review board to which he was unconnected.

Being a challenger is sometimes a humbling experience. Agility frequently cannot evolve from any single brilliant individual. It is almost always social, and it needs friends. Challengers must be willing to give away the credit for their ideas for them to advance. Perhaps the most significant finding we discovered as we were researching successful ideas was what we found with the unsuccessful ones. When we asked, "Please tell us about who else was engaged in helping to create a brilliant idea," we were given a plethora of names. Then, when we followed this lead and asked the same question, we were given additional names.

However, when we asked the inverse question, "Tell us about an idea you liked as much or maybe even more that wasn't adopted," something surprising happened. Nearly every time, we would get only a single name or two. When we met with these people, they weren't able to share any other names. Instead, they spent their time responding by raging against the "idiot" leaders or the "bureaucratic" processes that hindered the advancement of their idea. The contrast between successful and unsuccessful ideas was stark. Successful ideas had many friends and associates. Challengers seem to understand this innately and they seed and engage the network accordingly.

FIGURE 5.2 Seeding Across the Network

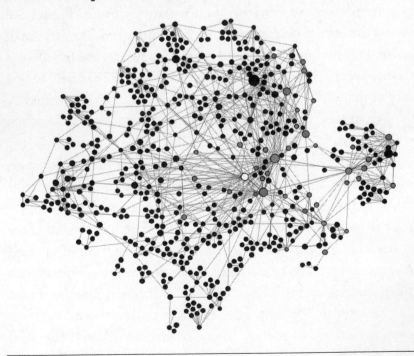

Crafting Disruption Connections

Brokers discover, connectors develop, and energizers diffuse. Challengers provoke disruption to usher in a new normal. They pay attention to external pressures and leverage them to catalyze agility. Like Jeff Bezos, they take a long view of success and power through the short-term distress. They create positive disruption connections that evolve into the creative destruction of the status quo. Challengers also extend beyond authoritative obedience and encourage constructive dissent. There are four essential ways to facilitate disruptive connections:

1. **Partition off positive disruptors.** Challengers understand that they need to leverage the power of development connections by separating them from the core. They formally challenge these groups to deliver on critical milestones within specific time frames much like IBM's "dirty dozen." They recognize that it is always better to be the disruptor than the disrupted. They challenge others to usher in new possibilities, opening up Adaptive Space for positive disruption to emerge.

2. **Confront conventional thinking.** Challengers acknowledge that current success contains the seeds for creative destruction. Unlike Motorola, they facilitate the connections necessary to facilitate the destruction of their own comfortable successes. They fight against the natural tendency of the "success syndrome" of getting locked in to conventional practices. They know that positive disruption is only the beginning and that a new normal must also be established.

3. **Encourage constructive dissent.** Challengers understand the destructive effects of obedience. They fight against the conformity that emerges within social groups throughout an organization. They encourage constructive dissent to fight against social control. They break down the division of "us" and "them" thinking by challenging groups.

4. **Seed the network for disruption.** Challengers understand how to leverage the power of connections. They understand how to break through social bubbles by seeding the network. They understand how to create network echo by getting those closest to them excited about new ideas and concepts.

Challengers build disruptive connections that fully leverage the power of networks. They leverage the discovery connections of brokers, the development interactions of connectors, and the diffusion connections of energizers to provoke disruption. Challengers therefore, open up Adaptive Space to create a new normal.

By recognizing the benefits of brokers, connectors, energizers, and challengers, organizations are able to facilitate critical connections. They can also facilitate these critical connections by employing five Adaptive Space principles: Organizations can discover by engaging the edges, develop by finding a friend, diffuse by following the energy, and disrupt by embracing the conflict. Finally, organizations need to actively set boundaries to close the network and facilitate Adaptive Space.

PART 2

Opening Up Adaptive Space

6

———●———

Engage the Edges

*There's no map for you to follow and
take your journey. You are Lewis and
Clark. You are the mapmaker.*

—PHILLIPA SOO

Without a map and with nothing to follow except courage
and a desire to discover, Meriwether Lewis and William
Clark set sail northward up the Missouri River on May 14,
1804, to find the elusive Northwest Passage. The exploration was
chartered by President Jefferson himself in hopes of discovering
a water route across the continent for the purposes of commerce,
with additional objectives ranging from botany to ethnogra-
phy. The 3,700 miles from the Mississippi River to the Pacific
Ocean on boat, horseback, and foot would prove to be a difficult and exciting journey into uncharted territories. They would
travel through impassable rivers filled with rapids and waterfalls,
encounter the ferocious grizzly bear, nearly freeze and starve to

death, and confront countless hostile situations, with the Black-feet trying to steal their weapons and the Crow taking half of their horses. They endured all of this in the pursuit of discovery.

Lewis and Clark took tremendous risks to journey well beyond the known edges of the North American continent. Their list of discoveries and creations were successful by any measure of exploration: producing maps for future explorers, developing an understanding of Indian culture, observing and documenting zoological and botanical knowledge, recording the meteorology of the West, and identifying many new species including the grizzly bear, prairie dog, and mountain goat. Perhaps most important, however, they spurred further curiosity in others to wander to the edge of the vast American West.

Today, organizations must discover their way through uncharted territory in a manner much like Lewis and Clark. Just consider Netflix's journey. Netflix had to enter into the wilderness of DVDs by mail, then it created the map for movie streaming, and now it is creating original content. With a desire to discover, organizations must embark upon a journey to the edge. Agility is dependent on these new discoveries. Social scientists suggest that brokers, who provide a bridge from one group to another inside an organization, act as conduits of discovery at the intersections of networks, or at the edges. The problem, however, is that in most organizations, brokerage is left to chance. That is, it may or may not occur based on individual actions. To remain competitive, organizations must deliberately enable discovery connections, and to do so, they must be more intentional in recognizing brokers and enabling Adaptive Space to engage the edges.

The challenge is that organizations are designed to move in the other direction—away from the edges, toward safety and predictability. As organizations mature, they have a tendency to become more and more insular, leaning into the operational system. The result is a building up of bureaucratic processes and structures that aim to reduce risks and uncertainties, creating a more fortified operational system that serves to protect the institutional assets. The unintended consequence is entrenchment in the status quo.

Agile organizations do something else. They make sure brokers gain access to diverse information and novel ideas from the edges. By doing so, new insights emerge to enable agility. They tap into the competitive advantages of brokers and leverage them to scan, connect, and discover both externally and internally. As highlighted in Chapter 2, brokers are essential to ensuring effective Adaptive Space. They provide bridges to discovery and help overcome insularity.

Sociologist Ron Burt's research on structural holes illustrates the power of these bridge connections in overcoming insularity.[1] A structural hole is present in networks when a gap exists between two groups. Information, ideas, and behavior are often isolated within these groups. Bridging structural holes therefore, is essential to discovery. These structural holes exist within organizations, perhaps as two different teams, operating as distinct entrepreneurial pockets. They can also exist outside of organizations, as two different institutions that could significantly benefit from each other's experience. Burt's research suggests that individuals on the edge of these holes are best positioned to have insightful ideas. These individuals have the potential to act as brokers, connecting groups and therefore being exposed to alternative ways of thinking and behaving. Brokers create bridges across structural holes. The result is they are exposed to more ideas, insights, and information from which to select and synthesize.

Burt suggests that social entities rich in structural holes, or having many edges, operate as entrepreneurial networks and are therefore more agile. In one case, he studied the value of ideas in a supply chain organization of 673 managers within a firm. Burt found that the value of any given idea corresponded to the degree in which a manager was bridging these structural holes. That is, the more managers bridged the edges of other groups, the more valuable their ideas were. These social exchanges on the edge become the lifeblood for agility. These edges therefore become fertile territory for innovative solutions to be revealed. Organizations can't rely solely on the possibility that brokers will bridge these holes, however. They need to more actively facilitate brokerage by enabling Adaptive Space.

Forging External Conduits

Procter & Gamble has long been regarded as a world-class global research and development organization. With thousands of scientists working in research centers across the world, P&G has experienced historical success by innovating from within and hiring the best in human capital. P&G was a consumer products behemoth, inventing such products as Tide laundry detergent, Crest toothpaste, Downy fabric softener, and Pampers diapers. The company created a science around evaluating the risks and results of innovation, whereby clear and measurable criteria for commercial success were explicitly managed. Indeed, P&G relied on superior internal capabilities and a small network of trusted partners to invent, develop, and deliver new products with tremendous success. Nevertheless, it became clear that this approach would not be the company's recipe for the future.

Over time, the costs of sustaining high levels of top-line growth outpaced the returns, and the explosion of new technologies began to level the external playing field. Small and midsize entrepreneurial companies were becoming increasingly more proficient at innovating. Information sharing and technical advancements were unfolding at unmatched speeds, and the race to market with exciting ideas and superior consumer products became increasingly more competitive.

Times had changed. In a hyperconnected world, millions of scientists, engineers, and entire companies suddenly began to have global access to one another and P&G had to respond. One study estimated that for every internal P&G researcher there were 200 researchers in the world who were just as good, creating a total pool of more than 1.5 million innovators.[2] They had to start thinking about how to engage the edges and move beyond the company's natural response of "proudly invented here" and shift toward an attitude of "proudly found elsewhere." They needed to actively scout for new ideas.

To do this, P&G embarked on a mission called "connect + develop" by systematically searching for proven technologies, packages, and products that could enhance its innovation efforts. P&G leaders knew they had to bridge structural holes, or they had to "broker + develop," which is a more accurate program name. P&G decision makers were very deliberate about engaging the edges and strategically evaluating exactly what they were looking for and where they wanted to play. They weren't interested in seeking an abundance of ideas; they were interested in marketable products, useful technologies, and necessary trademarks that would fill existing gaps.

Since its implementation, P&G's connect + develop program has discovered a number of key innovations from outside the organization and brought them inside. The discovery connections approach has been delivering superior products, faster than the conventional approaches, by enhancing or expanding existing projects with outside insights. It has also increased agility. P&G top executives recognized that they couldn't corner the market on good ideas. But, by engaging the edges, they could enable the connections necessary for good ideas to flow into the organization. When an idea, a technology, or a product fits a business goal or strategy, a thorough, confidential process of connecting with the idea originator is launched. If this due diligence process yields a fit, they begin working on a win-win partnership arrangement.

The company is now able to bridge the structural holes to provide access to new technologies, products, and processes when a need arises. For a number of years, P&G's skin care organization, for example, had been searching for a new anti-wrinkle technology for the next generation of Olay products. While attending a technical scouting conference in Europe, skin care researchers became aware of a new peptide technology that was developed by a small cosmetics company in France. P&G was so interested in the research that it invited the firm to share its entire set of data on the anti-wrinkle effects of the new peptide. The company accepted the invitation, and the new peptide became a key component in P&G's blockbuster product Olay Regenerist.

Engaging the edges and filling in structural holes has proven to be fruitful for P&G in discovering new solutions. Connect + develop has created new disciplines for noticing existing gaps and deliberately seeking external capacities to fill the voids, enhancing P&G's ability to actively shift toward new opportunities. Adaptive Space encourages organizations to design external discovery connections. These exchanges are rich in generating new insights, learning, and ideas, often resulting in bold new products for the company. While this program certainly hasn't been a panacea for P&G, and it continues to face strong head-winds in a challenging sector, P&G has created the capability to bridge external structural holes. By engaging the edges, it has demonstrated the courage and desire to discover like Lewis and Clark. P&G innovators have become mapmakers.

In a noteworthy study, Harvard professor Lee Fleming examined whether network position could enhance creativity.[3] He defined creativity as combining existing ideas in unexpected ways, calling them "novel combinations." A single patent that combined two different types of technology for the first time exemplifies these combinations. Fleming then evaluated the network structure that surrounded the authors of these novel combinations. He found that brokers, individuals who bridged across structural holes, were more likely to be part of novel com-binations. Furthermore, these structural holes did not mean that individuals from one group weren't aware of those from the other. It simply meant that they were so focused on their own activities that they weren't connected to the other group. P&G's connect + develop program, however, exploits this knowledge by intention-ally designing discovery connections to create Adaptive Space.

Of course, creating external conduits does not always have to be as methodical as connect + develop. Just consider Face-book's recent success with its "copy and paste" formula, where it has shrewdly mimicked some of Snapchat's most popular fea-tures.[4] Albeit some might think of this as a heist, others consider it a brilliant strategy. Facebook operates four of the most pop-ular apps in the world: Instagram, Messenger, WhatsApp, and the core Facebook app. It is already in a dominant position with an unprecedented number of users. This affords the opportunity to simply sit back and let others place bets on risky features. Facebook is then able to pluck out the most successful ones and incorporate them onto an existing platform. For example, all four of Facebook's major apps have integrated some variation of the Snapchat "Stories" feature into their design. Another example of the copy and paste strategy is the numerous Messenger features that first showed up on Apple's iMessage and Slack. In addition there is location sharing, which was first pioneered by Instagram Live.

Mark Zuckerberg and Facebook have been discovering innovations for some time now by connecting with their competitors' users. Twitter brought the "follower" feature, Foursquare offered the first "check in" capabilities, and Vine showcased short videos. All of these are now embedded into Facebook, and while some might argue that this approach is not constructive, Facebook recognizes that agility isn't about invention. It is about bringing usefulness into the world and quickly scaling it into a massive network.[5]

When you step back and look at the bigger picture, it is hard to dispute the impact of this strategy. Zuckerberg has agilely turned the company into a media and advertising powerhouse, all in the shadows of Google's success. Many have questioned the strategy, but Facebook has emerged as a multidimensional technological juggernaut that continues to place big bets. The copy and paste formula has enabled Zuckerberg to protect and grow the core business while freeing up resources to invest in the future of worldwide connectivity, augmented reality, and artificial intelligence. The combination of homegrown apps, copy and paste features, and big bets has enabled Facebook to engage the edges and remain agile while producing stellar results.

Perhaps more than ever, large organizations are best positioned to exploit these edges. They engage in many diverse connections with customers, suppliers, and partners. Just like P&G, they operate in numerous markets and interact with a multitude of entities. However, unlike Facebook, most companies' processes, structures, and work practices rarely enable such discoveries, and instead they remain insular, focused on daily performance. To remain competitive, organizations must enable intentional connections for discovery. Companies like Facebook and P&G have figured out how to engage the edges. They create connections to gain access to diverse information and novel ideas. The result is the potential for greater agility by bringing new ideas into the organization.

Finding Front Edge Users

Scientists have long marveled at how life flourishes on the edge where the sea thrusts upon the shore, creating the tidal pools. A diverse set of life-forms from mussels, to sea stars, to crabs and anemones lurk in beds of kelp and sea grass. These life-forms engage in a daily feast of food and oxygen. Algae and other intertidal plants grow in the abundant sunlight of the shallow waters, and the constant wave action supplies a rich source of nutrients and oxygen. Amidst pounding waves and powerful tides, these plants and animals are placed at great risk as they are frequently exposed to extreme conditions, such as summer's broiling sun or winter's freezing winds. The result of these edge exchanges is that more life originates and more mutations unfold in the tidal pool than any other place on earth. The same is true for agility; extreme edge users offer a richness of possibilities

133

that simply doesn't exist in the safe havens of day-to-day organizational existence.

Adaptive Space can act as a tidal pool that engages the extreme edge users—the geeks and freaks that live in the tidal pools of our world. These individuals have retrofitted or hacked products for their personal benefit, or perhaps they are using services for completely different reasons than their intended design. These are the people far from the center of the bell curve where the typical customer resides. They are often ignored because of their strange perspective or use, and yet they remain an incredibly valuable conduit for insight and learning based on their unusual perceptions. By connecting with extreme users of a given solution, we are often able to better understand undeveloped needs. That is, we can gain a deeper understanding of users' needs by looking for shortcuts they have created or by examining how they have repurposed products.

A good example of this is found with mountain bike users, who sought to take their bikes onto mountain terrain and began creating their own solutions, well in advance of the bicycle industry, in order to do so. Traditional commercial bikes were not designed for rough terrain, so these extreme users began retrofitting their bikes with wider tires to provide better traction and makeshift brake drums to enhance their ability to stop. These edge users who designed mutant bikes for off-road adventure became the fertile terrain for agility within the biking domain that ultimately led to an entirely new industry. Indeed, entrepreneurship researchers Nikolaus Franke and Sonali Shah found that more than one-third of individuals who belong to extreme sports clubs have developed or modified commercial products, thus serving as rich tidal pools.[6]

By engaging extreme users, organizations are able to discover the future today, building bridges to new possibilities. Just consider 3M as one example. Researchers within the company were very interested in infection control, so they identified some extreme cases that fell beyond their target market.[7] They looked at leading veterinary hospitals that had infection rates lower than those of some of the best human hospitals. They connected with military MASH units, where infections were historically low in spite of the fact that they weren't able to frequently scrub the fabric walls and dirt floors with antiseptic solutions. Finally they looked at movie makeup artists. Materials used by makeup artists are combined with latex so that they stick to the skin effectively but come off easily. The result of these reviews of edge users was that 3M discovered a set of unexpected and revolutionary new insights and radically different approaches to infection control problems, thus leading to identification of entirely new markets. For example, 3M now offers a full portfolio of hand hygiene products for various healthcare settings. Furthermore, 3M's studies proved that by creating Adaptive Space on the edges, organizations are able to more actively explore for new discoveries.

With methodologies like design thinking, organizations are able to create discovery connections between employees and extreme users. Just consider the automotive industry. By engaging people who can't, won't, or don't drive, new discoveries can emerge. For example, if you consider mobility for an aging population from a distance, you could inaccurately conclude that an Uber-like service might be an ideal solution to enabling elderly people to get around. However, by engaging in the interviewing techniques of design thinking, you will quickly recognize that the fear associated with getting into a car with a stranger is often overwhelming to an elderly person. Or, you might find that the physical assistance needed to get in and out of the vehicle creates a significant barrier for the driver. By leveraging the interviewing and observation techniques of design thinking, we can create deeper connections with the mobility needs of the aging population. The result is that entirely different solutions can then emerge.

Many organizations do not utilize techniques such as design thinking, however. Instead, they have become complacent in designing solutions from a distance, focused on the center of the bell curve. In one research case, a senior banking executive was invited to participate in an Adaptive Space interaction with the underbanked, or those who limit their use of banks for an assortment of reasons. The executive's first response was, "Why would I want low-income people as customers?" After much persistence, however, the executive finally relented and participated in a field visit. She quickly recognized that there were many Hispanic neighborhoods where residents' experiences and attitudes led to widespread distrust of banks. People thought banks would use their money for their own selfish interests and then charge them exorbitant fees. The executive recognized that many of these potential customers were budding entrepreneurs with significant funding needs that limited their businesses' growth. If leaders want to discover opportunities and create more agile organizations, they need to step outside of their own insular perspectives. They need to become discoverers like Lewis and Clark, traveling to the edge of the current organization and exploring new possibilities.

Organizations can also design discovery connections with edge users as a means for brokering new discoveries, generating avenues for users to influence adaptations. For example, an edge user invented the Twitter hashtag. When Twitter was launched in 2006, it was designed to provide a simple way to send text messages to large groups in 140 characters or less (since increased to 280 characters). There was never any intention of creating a text classification system for posts. It was designed to be elementary. The very word *Twitter* was selected because it referred to short burst of inconsequential information. However, thanks to a tweet by Chris Messina, an edge user, the hashtag concept using the # symbol was born.[8] Messina pitched the concept to an online community, being monitored by Twitter, as a way to organize messages into meaningful groups. From that point forth, Twitter users, as well as other online users, have embraced hashtags worldwide as the primary means to categorize information. Today, when you tweet a hashtag, it automatically becomes a clickable link. Anyone can click on it to find a page featuring the most recent tweets from that specific hashtag. As organizations like Twitter engage edge users like Messina, they create the Adaptive Space necessary to evolve.

Insights Hatched in Mixing Chambers

One way of intentionally facilitating brokerage is through the creation of mixing chambers, spaces where people can both connect and share. Mixing chambers intentionally facilitate brokerage connections by inviting the edges to join one another. During the discovery cycle, cadenced events, physical space, and ongoing affiliations can create a super broker fest. That means bringing people together for the sole purpose of engaging, sharing, and exchanging to discover.

One of the more remarkable mixing chambers is the MIT Media Lab. The Media Lab is a unique entity that resides on the edges of academia, research, and corporations. It is a place where the future is lived, not just imagined. Unconstrained by traditional discipline boundaries, the Media Lab engages product designers, nanotechnologists, data visualization experts, industry researchers, and pioneers of computer interfaces to work side by side to invent and reinvent a wide array of technology-centric activities that enhance everyday human experiences. The Media Lab is truly an interdisciplinary incubator that engages specialists from a variety of fields. Corporate sponsors represent an assortment of industries from electronics to entertainment, furniture to finance. The Media Lab is a living, dynamic exploration that extends well beyond traditional boundaries in an effort to continually scout for new insights and practical solutions.

The Media Lab also operates as an intellectual free-trade zone. Just consider the outcomes. Innovations include such inventions as the electronic ink technology that enables Amazon's Kindle, the large-scale data analytics that powers Twitter, and the machine learning platform that drives Spotify. Countless spin-off corporations and nonprofits have been generated as a result of the free-trade zone of the Media Lab. It is a mixing chamber for highly diverse groups and individuals to gather in an effort to discover. It is a living, collaborative environment that blends insights and ideas across many disciplines, fields, and industries. On the edge, where multiple entities engage, new possibilities can and do emerge. Deep within the main structures of institutions, such possibilities are often strangled out, but on the edge, they thrive. They're hacked, remixed, and invented. Such a free-trade zone encourages the birth of more radical adaptations.

Exchanges on the edge, or mixing chambers, can also be facilitated internally. For example, General Motors is transforming itself by generating brokerage relationships with its executive leaders. For the past few years, the company has partnered with Stanford University in running a yearlong Transformational Leadership program to spur innovative thinking. Groups of executives from different parts of the globe and different business functions are being brought together for a year to form a cohort designed to break down the once siloed culture. These cohorts represent 35 to 40 executives who participate in five intensive learning weeks together. During this time, they engage in traditional learning on such topics as customer-focused innovation, critical analytical thinking, and ambidextrous leadership. The mindset behind this program is very much concerned with how they can start to challenge themselves to think like a start-up, yet leverage the global footprint of the company. The executives also rotate locations for these five sessions, in such places as Detroit, Silicon Valley, Germany, Brazil, and China. Each of these locations offers new edges to visit and engage with. For example, in Silicon Valley the group members engage with the start-up community, in China they study emerging competitors, in Germany they evaluate emerging technologies, and in Brazil they partner with government officials and other multinational organizations to better understand fiscal policies. Finally, back in Detroit, they engage with the GM C-suite.

Perhaps the most significant part of this program, however, is the social capital that is established. These leaders certainly know or at least know of one another prior to their cohort experience. However, the bonds that are generated through a yearlong experience extend far beyond the formal program. The Stanford program forges broker relationships that span across silos. Participants build bridges that enable them to solve complex challenges in the future. They have also been able to sustain these relationships over time. For example, Figure 6.1 shows the evolution of connections for one of the cohorts. The first network shows the initial set of connections prior to the program. While connections existed, they were relatively sparse for such a senior group within the same company. The second diagram representing the end of the program shows the number of connections had tripled. However, the most important view is the final network diagram, two years after the conclusion of the program. It shows the majority of the connections have been maintained. Furthermore, new working brokerage relationships have been forged. These relationships have manifested themselves into bold new cross-functional innovations for such businesses as Cadillac, Maven, and Chevy.

FIGURE 6.1 Transformational Leadership Network

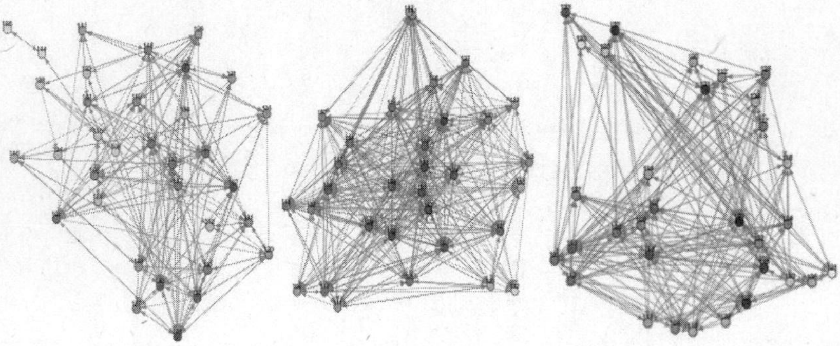

The program has also provided more immediate impact. At the end of the educational segments, a cohort is divided into five cross-functional teams and provided with a significant business challenge. Each team spends a few months leveraging the methods taught throughout the program to more deeply explore these challenges and come up with innovative business solutions. At the conclusion of their time together, each team pitches its ideas and implementation strategies on the emerging issue to Mary Barra and her team. The result is a set of bold, provocative solutions. In fact, innovations have been launched around concepts such as car sharing business models, self-driving vehicles platforms, vehicle exchange programs, and enhanced dealership experiences. The program has enabled the Adaptive Space necessary for bold changes to emerge.

Physical space design can also be leveraged to enable discovery connections. About a block away from the MIT Media Lab is the Stata Center.[9] This strange-looking $300 million building was designed with a very clear intent: to act as a mixing chamber on campus. The aim was that people would cross edges of various scientific disciplines, something highly unusual in academia, in order to collectively spawn great ideas. The complex was designed by famed architect Frank Gehry to increase the likelihood of edge interactions. Accordingly, in order to enhance the odds for effective chance encounters, the center is organized into neighborhoods vertically arranged throughout the building. The intent is to encourage faculty members and other researchers to interact with those in different scientific disciplines, rather than just back and forth on their own primary research floor. In other words, the design requires that researchers cross paths with other researchers while traveling within their own neighborhood. The centerpiece of this design is Student Street, an indoor walkway that bends and twists through the Stata's ground floor. The two major entrances to Student Street were designed to channel traffic from one side of the building to the other, acting as the only major walkway from one street to the next. The pathway, which incorporates a coffee shop, a fitness center, and a childcare center, winds through the building and is intermittently narrow, wide, high, and low. It also incorporates benches and tables, inviting individuals to stop and chat for a while, and there are even blackboards randomly located throughout the space, in the event that someone inspired by a breakthrough idea needs to write it down and share.

As you stop and watch for a while, you will notice many students and faculty rushing by, as they would at any university, and yet, over time, you begin to see huddles of brainstorming students gathering, and it is not unusual to see faculty members joining in and exchanging with the students as well. Indeed, rather than the usual instance of passing each other with the casual "Let's get together for coffee," the Stata design enables students and faculty to step aside from the busy human traffic patterns and actually get that coffee and sit down in a nook to share a thought or two.

The Stata's external appearance is a metaphor for the freedom and creativity intended to emerge from the inside of the mixing chamber. The walls seem to hover, swerve, and collide in random curves and angles in an almost whimsical manner, and a collective of unrelated parts and materials have been incorporated, including tan brick, brushed aluminum, brightly colored paint, and corrugated metal. It feels like a random array of textures and surfaces thrown together as an afterthought, and it serves beautifully as a symbolic illustration that diversity enhances creativity.

The Stata Center is not without criticism, however. The unconventional walls and radical angles have been the object of complaint, and from a conventional architecture or operational system perspective, the design is inefficient, with underutilized dead space and highly congested bottlenecks in tight quarters. Such deficiencies could drive a traditional architect mad. But, then again, most buildings aren't designed to be mixing chambers. Perhaps this is best exemplified by the outside amphitheater. On the south side of the building, facing the morning sun, is an amphitheater that appears to be rarely used in any formal capacity. It terraces up the side of the building for four stories, and upon observation, the amphitheater seems to be a space for socializing, picnicking, or just hanging out. But when you take a tour of the building, the amphitheater is described as an open space with easy access, designed to stage the next revolutions in scholarship, technology, and social trends. Indeed, it appears that MIT isn't leaving agility to chance; the potential for emergence has been intelligently incorporated into the Stata Center's design.

Curating Solutions from Within

Another powerful way of engaging the edge is the use of Adaptive Positive Deviance (APD). APD is predicated on the core premise that every community or organization has examples of individuals or small groups whose uncommon and unique practices result in superior outcomes. As Sharon Benjamin, along with her colleagues from Plexus Institute, describes it, "APD is a process focused on discovering and proactively developing unique, positive, and often subtle *differences* throughout a community that can generate new options and solutions. Looking to the community, not to outside experts, for data, engagements, insights, and solutions, APD emphasizes collaboration and community-wide practice. The emerging options for dealing with challenges are developed and understood through a shared community context."[10]

Jasper Palmer, a patient transport employee at Albert Einstein Medical Center in Philadelphia, serves as a great example of APD in action. He noticed that the protective gowns and gloves that staff wore often overflowed from the hospital's disposal bins onto the floor, and he devised his own method to address the issue. When Palmer took off his gown, he "rolled it up into the size of a baseball and pulled his gloves over it to contain it in a tight package." Within most organizations, that would have been the end of the story. However, the Einstein Medical Center had launched an organization-wide effort to fight the spreading of methicillin-resistant *Staphylococcus aureus* (MRSA) through the use of a strategy called positive deviance. The intent was to connect dozens of small ideas and insights that emerged from countless interactions and encounters that take place every day. Indeed, "Positive deviance is a bottom-up, rather than top-down, approach, to solving prevalent, seemingly intractable problems. . . . It's based on the observation that, in most communities, certain individuals and groups (positive deviants)" often find or develop highly effective solutions to difficult problems.[11]

The Einstein Medical Center engaged the edges by connecting nurses, physicians, and staff in a quest to find these solutions, and as part of this effort, a nurse recalled Jasper Palmer's demonstration of de-gowning. She remembered how he would slide out of the gown, twirl it around his right arm, and stuff it into his glove. This discovery proved to not only be effective in dealing with the overflowing trash bins, but also a highly effective way of thwarting germs such as MRSA, and has since been widely adopted as the "Palmer Method." By connecting hundreds of hospital staff members, environmental services staff, nurses, physical therapists, recreational therapists, unit secretaries, physicians, residents, and even patients, the Einstein Medical Center has uncovered numerous practices to prevent the transmission of MRSA. It has tapped into a vast network of brokers and created discovery exchanges internally.

Internal insights do not exclusively have to be discovered from positive deviance. They can also be intentionally cultivated on the edges. Entrepreneurial pockets, partitioned off on the fringe of a company, enable discoveries to be introduced as needed. Just consider the Coca-Cola Founders Platform. The company has been investing in a number of promising entrepreneurs to generate future financial growth for the organization and to discover solutions to challenging business problems such as product restocking and marketing to millennials. Coke operates these start-ups as separate, independent, semi-connected entities that function as entrepreneurial pockets connected through brokers. Coke recognizes that partitioning them off enables speed and agility.

It is important to note that originally the program pulled the start-up founders inside the core organization and paired them with Coke mentors. Leaders quickly realized, however, that the entrepreneurs were constrained by the corporate bureaucracy. Coke's rules and processes stifled them, so the company quickly decided to let the start-ups operate semi-independently and to simply curate learnings from them.[12] For example, a founder's partner from Australia helped Coke to discover a breakthrough for restocking vending machines. The number of empty vending machines had been a chronic problem, and the discovery connections with the start-up helped to enhance revenue per machine by 27 percent and reduce restocking deliveries by 21 percent. Both were monumental improvements over previous practices.

Connections with another founder start-up, Wonolo, generated a solution that addressed the problem of lost sales from out-of-stock products in retail stores. Coke's preference was to restock a shelf the moment it's empty, but retailer staffing models don't always allow for that. Wonolo, however, created an app that matches retailer needs for stocking with people seeking temporary work. The app enables a retailer to post a temporary job to a prescreened group of workers, or "Wonoloers." Job seekers are then able to accept a job they are interested in, much in the same manner as an Uber driver, with average time to fill a job being only four minutes, which is much faster than using a temporary staffing service, thus creating greater agility. Even more exciting is that the cost of this approach is 40 percent less than that of traditional staffing solutions.

Companies like P&G, Facebook, 3M, and Coke are engaging the edges to construct conduits of discovery to find new ideas. They establish bridges across structural holes, creating fruitful social exchanges on the edge. By facilitating brokerage connections on the edges, organizations are then able to get there early, much in the same manner as Lewis and Clark.

There are five core strategies for engaging the edges for critical discoveries:

1. **Map out the edges.** Organizations need to actively journey through uncharted territory. They need to generate strategy landscape maps for the future, ahead of the competitors, in the same manner that Netflix did with DVDs by mail, streaming movies, and then creating original content.

2. **Search the tidal pools.** Organizations also need to navigate beyond existing users and engage the extreme edge users to discover new possibilities. They need to use techniques like design thinking to gain a deeper understanding of user needs and to look for analogous solutions in the same manner as 3M.

3. **Design deliberate space.** Organizations need to intentionally design physical space as a means for enabling discovery connections. They need to consider creative arrangements that will encourage serendipity in the same manner as the MIT Stata Center.

4. **Find the positive deviants.** Much like the Einstein Medical Center, organizations need to seek out positive deviants. They need to focus on discovering "unique, positive, and often subtle differences throughout a community that can generate new options and solutions."[13]

5. **Cultivate pockets.** Organizations need to cultivate pockets on the edges, in the same manner as the Coca-Cola Founders Platform. They need to partition off critical bets to enable discoveries to be introduced as needed and to connect these entrepreneurial pockets with brokers.

7

Find a Friend

*A friend is someone who gives you
total freedom to be yourself.*

—Jim Morrison

ave Myers had an idea to create and apply a polymer to the
gears of his mountain bike so he could shift more smoothly
as he was climbing hills.[1] Myers was used to ascending the
steep hills in Flagstaff, Arizona, where he worked at the W.L.
Gore & Associates medical-products facility, which was devoted
to the development and manufacturing of implantable medical devices. This was an unlikely place for innovations to bicycle
gear cables. However, Myers worked for a company that encourages its associates to spend time on speculative new ideas inside
entrepreneurial pockets. As a result, Myers was free to tinker
with solutions for his own mountain bike.

Myers's polymer product wasn't exactly a raving success.
However, when he turned to a friend, a real breakthrough

occurred. Fellow engineer and colleague Chuck Hebestreit was a guitarist who had personally experienced the frustration of sound distortion and the frequency of snapping strings. The grooves in traditional strings tended to accumulate oil and skin particles, which resulted in a dampening sound. Furthermore, the natural exposure to air caused string corrosion, contributing to their premature breakage. Hebestreit challenged his friend to consider an alternative application for his polymer creation and use it on guitar strings. After months of experimentation with only limited success, John Spencer, another friend, heard about their project, and joined Myers and Hebestreit. The trio then persuaded another half-dozen colleagues to help develop and experiment with the project in their spare time. After many months of testing, the self-organized group felt they had a product that made sense for consumers. Only then did they seek formal endorsement from the broader organization so they could take the product to market. It is important to note that until this point, because of Gore's encouragement toward entrepreneurial pockets, they had never needed to ask permission, seek financial resources, or ask for time off. They were encouraged to follow their own motivations, operating in the Adaptive Space necessary to connect, test, and iterate their idea in response to the challenge of many trials that didn't work. The result was a new product called Elixir, a top-selling acoustic guitar string, and perhaps Gore's biggest technological advance of the last three decades.

When innovators discover something important or compelling, their natural inclination is to quickly seek leadership support. They reason that if they can garner formal approval, they will be able to get their idea implemented sooner and scaled more broadly. This rarely works, however. Leaders, who are primarily responsible for managing the efficiencies of an operational system, are more inclined to shut down rough ideas than to blindly endorse them. Furthermore, most leaders are inundated with new ideas and suggestions, and they simply cannot support them all. A more effective strategy for getting these ideas formally endorsed, therefore, is to start by finding a friend to begin the development process, and when that works, to create the intentional interactions necessary to engage others, thus creating Adaptive Space.

This is exactly what happened when two junior engine calibration engineers within General Motors, Bailey Streicher and Andrew Kneifel, connected. After attending a GM2020 summit, Streicher had an idea: what if she ran a catalyst event for her location at the Milford Proving Grounds just outside Detroit? Intrigued with this possibility, she went and found a friend, Kneifel, who also attended the summit. The two of them began to brainstorm creative ideas that could make a difference locally and soon had generated enough buzz that others started to engage. The band of self-organized change agents met weekly to discuss possibilities, and ultimately, the duo (represented as the two light nodes in Figure 7.1) inspired the local network to take many small actions. Soon they had generated enough energy that local leadership began to notice, and it was only then that Streicher and Kneifel sought out executive support (the slightly larger black node left of center in Figure 7.1) to run a local catalyst event. Already intrigued by the local interest, leadership had little choice but to endorse the idea.

Soon after the event, numerous seemingly unrelated but important collaborative activities began to emerge across the network. One person started a local women's affinity group to encourage female engineers, two others decided to create a fun communications brief that highlighted local happenings, and yet another sponsored a local benefits session to encourage employees to get the most out of their opportunities. One young engineer also created a simple online idea exchange system to encourage others to engage by voting suggestions up or down. As the local network began to grow, leadership started to actively leverage the community to facilitate numerous employee engagement activities. Employees even went out and recruited food truck vendors to provide better eating options on campus. Streicher's and Kneifel's initial idea manifested into a band of change agents that created a local movement. As Streicher says, "A great idea can be stopped by a single no, but it can also be catapulted by one profound yes."

FIGURE 7.1 Streicher's Find a Friend Network

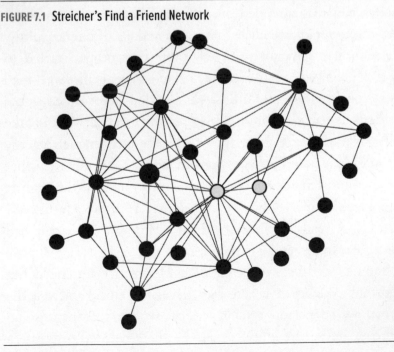

The value of an idea can only be realized through successful development. For organizations to be agile, it is critical to discover ideas and activities on the edges. However, to bring something to reality, they need to start locally and small. Brokers challenge the organization to think big by discovering new information, insights, and ideas by engaging the edges. However, ideas alone are cheap, often observed and tossed aside. Successful development starts by finding a friend.

The First Friend Effect

The inclination is to secure leadership support quickly. But finding a friend is much more likely to result in a yes that catapults an idea forward. We have many ideas, and often we aren't even sure ourselves which ones are good. Socialization with a friend offers an initial gut check of the surface merit of an idea, and it provides an initial perspective as to what to do next. Streicher didn't really know if her idea was good or if it was appropriate for the local site. Kneifel not only validated her idea, he enabled her to be bolder than she might have been if she had taken the idea directly to her leader. As Jim Morrison once said, "A friend is someone who gives you total freedom to be yourself." This freedom enables individuals to test even the boldest of ideas with a friend. We are social creatures, and we are always seeking acceptance for our ideas. Finding a friend to share the idea is the first step.

This is exactly what we found with one product development specialist inside a large financial service firm. She had built an impressive track record of market successes, and when we asked her why she was successful, her response was, "I always start in my safe zone, with those people that I most trust." Often she finds this friend within her entrepreneurial pocket. She went on to say, "There is minimal risk in sharing with a friend; they will tell me the truth if the idea is bad or they will encourage me to leap forward if it is good." Clearly the first friend plays a critical role in an idea's survival.

Derek Sivers introduced the power of this concept during his 2010 TED conference.[2] He showed a video of a single shirtless guy dancing alone in a field at a music festival. At first the guy looks like a drunken lunatic who needs some friends to settle him down. But then something amazing happens. The first follower enters the dance, and all of a sudden the lunatic's original idea, of dancing shirtless in the field, is beginning to look interesting to others. Soon, the second guy begins to wave others onto the scene, and while initially the bystanders looked at that shirtless man dancing alone as a nut, now they have become intrigued because for some inexplicable reason, two guys dancing in the field just isn't as crazy. As the video goes on, another person joins in, and then two more people join in. Soon, a band of dancing men and women is forged, making it far more comfortable for others to join in. This quickly turns into a crowd of dancing people across the field. As Sivers points out in his talk, it was the first follower who turned the shirtless lunatic into a brilliant creator. The first follower holds the power to transform an individual with a unique idea into a movement.

The same is true for the first friend. The person who introduces the idea will often get the credit, but it is the friend who validates the idea to others. This person reinforces the idea and encourages the creator to continue in the development process. Without a first friend, the idea will eventually dissipate—in other words, the dancer will give up. The friend actually emboldens the creator to double down on the idea. The first friend is also the one who draws others onto the scene, encouraging them to engage. Furthermore, first friends appear more trustworthy to others because they offer a more unbiased view. After all, it wasn't their idea to begin with, and yet they have freely chosen to invest in it. First friends also enhance the social equity of the idea's creator. They provide a kind of unbiased reference for the idea. The idea seems less weird or risky as a crowd begins to gather. As interests emerge from these interactions, the circle of friends is expanded and confidence to pursue the idea gains momentum.

Friends can also be active in the enhancement process. Not only do they embolden the originator and draw others to the idea, friends can also help develop the idea. This is exactly how the product Elixir was developed. Dave Myers's colleague, Chuck Hebestreit, the first friend, was the tipping point for the development process. Hebestreit didn't only embolden Myers's idea, he build upon it and catapulted it into an entirely different space, guitar strings. The duo then recruited a half-dozen colleagues to help build out the concept and join their little entrepreneurial pocket. Finally, when it was ready to be shared more broadly, their collaboration created the Adaptive Space necessary to diffuse the concept.

For many organizations, bottom-up innovations, like Elixir guitar strings, are the exception. Above all odds, a tenacious entrepreneur generates a new idea and risks everything in an attempt to gain formal leadership endorsement. Innovators within this model are forced to risk their reputations by engaging in a direct assault against the current operational system. Most individuals are not encouraged to find a friend and build up the social equity around an idea. However, unlike many companies, Gore was designed to operate in Adaptive Space. The company has always deliberately generated internal social capital. This originated back in 1958, when Bill L. Gore left DuPont to launch his own start-up. Gore was fond of saying that in a hierarchical company, "communication can only happen in the car pool."[3] Indeed, that was the only place associates would talk openly with no regard to repercussions from the chain of command.

Gore decided early on to toss aside the traditional rules of the hierarchy. Instead, he created a lattice organization that would encourage natural leadership rather than authority-based leadership. He argued, "Every successful organization has a lattice organization that underlies the facade of authoritarian hierarchy. It is through these lattice organizations that things get done." Accordingly, he designed an organization that enabled Adaptive Space well before others did, and he encouraged direct, one-on-one communication whereby any one person could communicate with anyone else to progress an idea. Even today, associates are encouraged to build development connections through their lattice, with the understanding being that every associate has a lattice, or a kind of personal network. It is associates' responsibility, therefore, to partner with others to build their own lattice and extend their own social capital throughout the organization. This level of connectivity provides a transparency for what others are working on, what skills they possess, and what interests exist. These development connections are invaluable for finding friends with whom to create innovative products.

W.L. Gore & Associates thus encourages its people to tap into the entrepreneurial pockets, finding friends before leaders. Adaptive Space is essential to this. Indeed, Gore associates are taught to morph their roles over time to match their particular skills and interests. The expectation isn't to act within the confines of a standard job description or top-down expectations. In contrast, Adaptive Space requires an environment where individuals can find safe havens to experiment and connect ideas.

Clearly, Gore is an agile company that prides itself on nurturing connections, which can result in technological breakthroughs such as Elixir, even when the company had no experience whatsoever in the music business. Indeed, Gore's aptitude for innovation didn't come from major investments in R&D, or from organizing around major challenges. Rather, it evolved from a culture that fostered Adaptive Space, encouraging individuals to nurture connections. Accordingly, associates feel free to create and pursue ideas on their own and to engage others, based on shared interests rather than solely defined responsibilities.

Follow and Feed Social Buzz

When a few friends, like Myers, Hebestreit, and Spencer, begin to work together on something, others take notice. None of us want to miss out on the next big thing. We want to be insiders. As a result, our tendency is to assume that if groups of people are interested in something, there is likely a good reason. Sociologists call this social proof. When individuals are not certain how to respond or what the outcome will be, they often look for cues from others. They will look for the social responses that indicate what others are thinking or doing. We often coalesce because we believe those around us have a more accurate response to an ambiguous situation, and so we follow. Social proof is especially powerful when another person is perceived as being particularly knowledgeable. So when small groups like Myers, Hebestreit, and Spencer are fervently working on something, others want to join. This is how movements begin. Eventually so many people join in that it becomes almost riskier to be a bystander.

Perhaps one of the most compelling demonstration of social proof in action is the famous street corner experiment. In 1968, social psychologists Stanley Milgram and his colleagues conducted an experiment around the idea of social influence in the streets of New York.[4] On two cold winter evenings, Milgram and a group of researchers engaged passing pedestrians in the experiment. They wanted to see what would happen if individuals stood on a busy street and looked up at the sixth floor of an adjacent office building where nothing of any significance was happening. First, they placed a single person on the corner and asked him to look up at the building for 60 seconds. A small fraction of the pedestrians stopped to see what the guy was looking at. Most simply ignored him and went on their way. Next the researchers instructed five individuals to stare up at the building, and the number of pedestrians who stopped and looked up quadrupled. Finally, the researchers instructed 15 individuals to stand on the corner and look up at the building. This time 86 percent of passersby looked up to see what was going on, proving that a small crowd of 15 people could have a significant influence on others under specific circumstances.

This is different from peer pressure or conformity. Individuals are not looking up at the building because of social status. They stop and notice because they assume something interesting must be happening. We look for social confirmation, and when we get it, we join in. This is exactly what happened with Apple's iPod. Prior to the iPod, headphone cords were black. However, Apple is masterful at creating social buzz, and its designers knew that the iPod would spend most of its time in people's pockets. Therefore, passersby would not know that someone was listening to an iPod. So Apple made the headphones white—a decision that proved to be brilliant.[5] It provided social proof that white earbuds evoked coolness and style. Of course, Apple leveraged this to the fullest extent possible with the silhouettes advertising campaign highlighting the white earbuds, and they, in turn, became the "tipping point" for the iPod.

When it comes to new ideas, a practical approach for evaluating social conformity is to build and share a prototype. Indeed, a major element of the design thinking process is prototyping. This method enables individuals to bring an idea to life in either a physical or experiential nature. Early, inexpensive prototypes provide the opportunity to quickly test an idea and evaluate it for social adaptation. A prototype is the first step to bringing a new solution into the world, and it gets the idea out of an individual's head and into a physical form that can be shared with others. For example, in one research case, a trio of designers inside a technology firm had an idea for a new software feature. They quickly sketched out a few interactive wireframes and started to socialize them with others inside the company. The trio immediately got positive feedback, with people saying, "I was thinking the same thing the other day" or "Wow, why didn't we think of that sooner." By creating a prototype, they were able to test for social proof before investing more valuable resources into the development process.

Seeking social proof could just as easily work in the opposite direction. We have been taught to believe if a crowd doesn't gather, it must not be interesting. Consider another example. On a cold Friday morning in January, during the middle of rush hour, a man pulled out his violin and positioned himself strategically between the top of an escalator and a major exit of the L'Enfant Plaza, in the center of Washington, D.C.[6] The violinist placed an open case near his feet with a few dollars as seed money and began to play what would be the first of his six classical pieces. He was wearing jeans, a long-sleeved T-shirt, and a Washington Nationals baseball cap, and he continued to play for a total of 43 minutes. During this time, 1,097 people passed by, most of them on their way to work. Only seven stopped long enough to actually take in the performance for at least a minute. Twenty-seven people gave money, most of them as they were running by, leaving a total of 1,070 people who hurried by, oblivious to the violinist.

No one seemed to notice that the man playing was Joshua Bell, the onetime child prodigy and internationally acclaimed virtuoso. Only three days before, he had filled the house at Boston's stately Symphony Hall, where average seats went for $100. Nor did anyone notice that Bell was playing a $3.5 million violin, handcrafted in 1713 by Antonio Stradivari during the Italian master's "golden period." No, the people in the plaza were too busy, intent on getting where they had to be. They couldn't notice the gift that had been presented to them on this cold morning.

When it comes to noticing, friends matter. If two or three people stop and notice something, others notice them noticing. It creates a different state of social attention, the ability to pause and observe what's unfolding. In our frenetic world, where hurriedness overrides stillness, this is even more important. It is commonplace to miss these opportunities. Social proof encourages individuals to operate as if they were seeing something for the very first time, unlike the passersby in the L'Enfant Plaza. A gathering of friends provides the evidence that something is worth considering. If Joshua Bell were really trying to be noticed, he would have brought some friends with him.

GM2020 was created on this notion. A small group of employees wanted to positively disrupt work within the large, complex organization. So rather than seeking formal endorsement or launching a formal initiative, they decided to invite a few friends to a two-day event designed to "reimagine the way we work." In all, 60 people showed up to engage in a conversation called a GM2020 Summit, aimed to "think big, but start small." At the conclusion of the event, participants were challenged to go find a friend and take action, no matter how small. They were also given two GM2020 badges, one for themselves to place over their building entry badge so that it was visible to others and one for their friend. Much like Apple's white earbuds, group members wanted to build social proof across the community that they were going to create a movement to reimagine work. Informally, friends engaged with each other to initiate local changes such as a job shadowing for employees, an internal career fair, a connection menu to help people better assimilate into teams, and even a talent exchange program so employees could get different experiences.

Finding a friend legitimized these changes to others, and soon small bands of employees were working on all kinds of local issues. The badges provided the social proof necessary for others to engage. Only three years later, members from the community sent out invitations to friends to participate in the third annual GM2020 Summit, and within 24 hours more than 1,000 employees signed up. It turns out that finding a friend and providing social proof make a difference.

Shaping Your Inner Circle

British anthropologist Robin Dunbar hypothesized that our friendships are layered. That is, as humans we have an inner and outer circle of friends that total on average 150, the "Dunbar

Number." He argued that this is the number of relationships that any single person can feasibly maintain based on the size of the human brain. To validate this hypothesis, researchers Pádraig MacCarron and Kimmo Kaski, along with Dunbar, conducted a more comprehensive study in 2007 to examine the layers of friendships.[7] They analyzed nearly 6 billion phone call records, of millions of people throughout Europe. By applying a clustering approach, they then stratified these calls into friendship layers. What they found was on average people are likely to have about four deep relationships, nearly seven slightly less intimate friends, about 20 semi-distant friends, and then another 100 friends in an outer circle. This leaves us with an inner circle of less than a dozen people. It is our inner circle of friends that most directly influences our behaviors.

Everyone has an inner circle of friends, family, colleagues, and advisors with whom they routinely engage. These are the people who either positively or negatively shape our views, perspective, and beliefs. Friends can either inspire or impede success. In his famous experiment in the 1950s, social psychologist Solomon Asch evaluated the impact that social pressure had on an individual's perception.[8] In an experiment, he asked a group of volunteers to match the length of a vertical black line on a plain white card to one of three different options on another white card. In small groups, volunteers would then reveal their choices, one after another. What Asch found was remarkable. Each person's choice was highly dependent on what others revealed first. That is, when individuals in the group overestimated the length, other individuals would follow suit. They also underestimated. In all, 37 of the 50 participants selected an "obviously erroneous" answer at least once during the experiment. Asch concluded that there is a strong social tendency for conformity. This is what happens within our inner circle, yet we rarely think about how to actively shape these relationships.

Successful individuals pull positive people into their inner circle. They surround themselves with people who are enthusiastic, optimistic, and generous. They are intentional about the kinds of relationships they are building. For example, one successful executive from our research created an advisory board that represented her inner circle. She was taking on an incredibly challenging role to turn around a floundering business, and she knew she would need their help. She literally selected friends based on their individual demeanors. One person was her "bold advisor" and was in charge of challenging her to make decisions that were 10 times bolder than was typical. Another person was her "change ambassador" and provided active advice on how to navigate the political landscape. She also had an "innovator" to drive growth and a "devil's advocate" to minimize the impact of risky decisions. The executive advisory board, all close friends, would actively provide personal guidance to her. From time to time, they would even get together in person to provide group guidance. With the support of her intentional inner circle, she was successful in helping to facilitate a significant turnaround of the business.

As Asch discovered, individuals have a strong social bias toward group conformity. More recent research suggests that this might have an involuntary component as well as a social element. The neural network in our brains becomes active as soon as we disagree with others. Perhaps worse yet, specific parts of a person's neural network are activated just before the person changes views to align with others. This inward shift begins social interactions, as people falsely agree with others. However, fMRI scans suggest that individuals quickly begin to rationalize their choices in response to social conformity, increasing the chances that they actually change their core beliefs.[9] In short, our friends can literally change our minds.

As we were warned as children, we need to be careful of the company we keep. Or maybe worse, the company that keeps us. We can learn a lot about ourselves by simply examining our inner circle. They change our beliefs. We become our network. No matter how brilliant and innovative a person is, he or she is predisposed to abandon the most entrepreneurial ideas in response to that inner circle. Our network reflects us. If we want to be agile, then those closest to us need to be agile.

A practical approach to creating agility in the local development process is to use the scrum method. Scrum teams are used frequently in software development. They usually represent small, tight-knit team members who are colocated with each other. The process forces rapid iteration into the development process to ensure agility. For example, the scrum method facilitates four "ceremonies" that bring structure to the process: planning, daily standups, demos, and retrospectives. These ceremonies force rapid iteration and synchronization in very short bursts of development. They fortify an inner circle by forging an entrepreneurial pocket of activity.

A great example of this is Netflix. Netflix.com is one of the most dynamic websites in the world. The site literally changes every two weeks, and most of the modifications don't work for users. However, the company believes in the freedom of fast iterations.[10] It uses a try and see approach, keeping what works and tossing aside what doesn't. The web-application team uses the scrum method. Fast iterations provide Adaptive Space for teams to quickly test many features and then build on those that generate social proof. As one designer said, "We make a lot of this stuff up as we go along." The team doesn't assume things will work without real-world tests. The web-application team has forged an inner circle of developers who challenge each other to test and iterate, ensuring agility.

Much like with the scrum method, Rob Cross's research proposes that we need to actively manage our network to ensure agility.[11] He suggests that individuals must stay focused on the "why" of the work, creating interactions that nurture a shared sense of purpose. Organizations must maintain an intense focus on development and build interactions with people who care about similar outcomes. They need to cocreate and iterate. They need to explore opportunities by engaging friends in the process early. If our inner circle reflects us, it is essential that we more intentionally select our friends. We need to shape our inner circle to facilitate agility.

Flying with Birds of a Feather

It has been said that opposites attract. This is more myth than reality. As social creatures, there is a tendency for individuals to be attached to other individuals who are similar to them. Sociologists call this tendency *homophily*, which simply means that people tend to form connections and build friendships with individuals who have similar interests, beliefs, or attitudes. These attractions have the capacity to rapidly form into new entrepreneurial pockets of activity. The perception of similarity improves coordination and agreement. Homophily creates a certain level of acceptance that accelerates social engagement. It helps people to access information from one another, and to share ideas openly based on positive trust. The old proverb that birds of a feather flock together can enhance responsiveness. Homophily enables groups to form together more quickly to address issues.

Consider Nucor Steel, for example.[12] At about two o'clock in the afternoon, multiple Nucor electricians got a call, bearing some bad news, from a fellow electrician from the Hickman, Arkansas facility. The facility's electrical grid had failed, which, for a steelmaker like Nucor, is one of the worst possible scenarios. Almost immediately, the electricians started traveling to Arkansas. One electrician, who was visiting a facility in Indiana, drove to Arkansas, arriving at nine o'clock that night. Two others quickly boarded a plane in North Carolina, landing in Memphis at 11 p.m., and then preceded to drive two hours to the troubled facility. Once the trio arrived, they worked 20-hour shifts to get the facility up and running again in three days instead of the anticipated full week. Perhaps the most amazing part of this illustration is that no one mandated that the trio travel to Arkansas so quickly. No, the three acted autonomously of their own accord as birds of the same feather. They were all electricians, and they could relate to the situation.

Nucor, the largest steel producer and recycler in the United States, with operating facilities in 14 states, is also known for its culture and its commitment toward its employees. Indeed, Nucor has consistently outperformed the industry over the last decade in an incredibly challenging market. Authors have thus frequently attributed the company's success to its culture, which includes only four management layers and seeks to minimize bureaucracy with a streamlined organizational structure. However, there is another reason. Nucor's philosophy is quite simple. It is based on a recruitment process that focuses on employing people with the right cultural fit, rather than people who could simply be highly skilled individual contributors. They seek birds of the feather.

There is another reason why the Nucor electricians felt compelled to move so quickly. They were asked to help, to provide a favor. A few years ago, researchers conducted an experiment illustrating this point.[13] Interested in better understanding motivational aspects of compensation verses social capital, they designed an elementary computer experiment, asking participants to drag a circle across the screen into a box by using a mouse. Participants were asked to repeat this task as many times as they could in a five-minute cycle, and the study was designed for three different tests. People in the first group were handed five dollars as they entered the lab and were told that at the end of five minutes the computer would alert them that the exercise was complete and they would be able to leave. The second group was provided the same instructions but received significantly less compensation (10 cents in one experiment and 50 cents in another). Finally, the third group wasn't offered any compensation. Instead, participants were asked to participate as a social request only, being asked to do the tasks as a favor.

The results proved surprising. As expected, the first group moved 159 circles, on average, whereby the second group, which received far less in compensation, only moved 101 circles. The third group, however, moved on average 168 circles. Remember, this was the group that had received no monetary reward. It seems that the social appeal was a more important motivator than the financial one. Accordingly, we can surmise that social capital matters. This was also true for the Nucor electricians. Building social capital and creating highly cohesive relationships helps drive agility.

As with Nucor, homophily can create a sense of safety that enables agility and speed. It can also help with creativity. Teresa Amabile, a professor at Harvard Business School, has conducted years of research in the area of creativity, and has developed a core hypothesis, formulated through a multitude of social-psychological experiments, that positive environments help enable greater creativity.[14] Amabile found that positive emotion was associated with higher creativity, and there seemed to be a constant interplay of perceptions, emotions, and motivations, triggered by daily events. People were more creative when they saw their environment as collaborative, cooperative, and open to new ideas, and they were over 50 percent more likely to have creative ideas on the days they reported having positive emotions. On the other hand, creativity was suppressed when political infighting or aversion to risk taking were high. Friends, more than anyone else, generate positive emotions. After all, this is why birds of a feather flock together.

Organizations like W.L. Gore and Associates, Netflix, and Nucor have embraced the finding a friend approach to organizational agility. They provide the freedom necessary for people to share, test, and iterate ideas. They enable individuals to socialize ideas and generate social buzz. In conclusion, there are five core strategies for finding a friend to create development connections:

1. **Engage the first friend.** Individuals need to share quickly with a first friend. They need to create an initial gut check around an idea and to tap into the ability of the first friend to draw others in, much as Bailey Streicher did with Andrew Kneifel.
2. **Build your lattice.** Individuals need to leverage their lattice to get things done. Much like associates at Gore, they need to engage in direct, one-on-one communication to progress their idea. They need to build their

lattice and extend their own social capital throughout the organization.

3. **Seed for social proof.** Individuals need to bring friends with them to the party to create a different state of social attention. They need to create an environment to seed social proof, which encourages people to engage, unlike the passersby in the L'Enfant Plaza.

4. **Forge your inner circle.** Individuals need to create an advisory board of friends who challenge them to be agile and provide active guidance. They need to surround themselves with a network that reflects their intentions.

5. **Create a scrum.** Individuals need to create a scrum team—a small, tight-knit group of friends who force rapid iteration into the development process. They need to create ceremonies that ensure planning, daily stand-ups, demos, and retrospectives.

8

Follow the Energy

People like to be around those who
give off positive energy.

—Erin Heatherton

In the fall of 2011, in a small town just outside of Buffalo, New York, something strange began to happen. Over a few weeks, 12 teenage girls from LeRoy Junior-Senior High School began to show symptoms similar to those of Tourette's syndrome.[1] The girls were twitching their arms, as they painfully shook their heads and jerked back and forth. The number of girls grew from 12 to 16, and finally to 18, and doctors were baffled. Officials began to look for infections, communicable diseases, and other environmental factors. However, the investigation showed no evidence of anything being out of the ordinary. Finally, after interviewing some of the girls, Dr. Laszlo Mechtler, a neurologist at the DENT Neurologic Institute in Amherst, New York, concluded that the girls had a type of conversion disorder that is sometimes referred to as mass hysteria. According to Dr. Mechtler, with treatment the girls would get better over time.

Researchers believe conversion disorder originates from an overactive amygdala, which is the emotional and fear response center of the brain. In this bizarre case, however, the question was how one person's conversion disorder could spread to another person's neural pathways. Scientists now believe that the regions in our brain once thought to spark only our own activity or sensations can actually impact those around us. Mirror neurons can fire both when we act and when we observe another person's action. The result is that the neurons "mirror" the observed behavior. It is a kind of empathy that finds expression in actions, such as a contagious yawn or sympathetic pain.

Regardless of how this happens, one thing can't be disputed. Group conversion disorder, or mass hysteria, seems to be contagious from friend to friend. In 1983, over 900 Palestinian teenage girls fainted or complained of feeling nauseous in the West Bank of Israel.[2] Officials eventually concluded that the wave of complaints was ultimately a product of mass hysteria. Then in 1988, the U.S. Navy evacuated 600 men from their barracks in San Diego after complaints of difficulty breathing. Investigators found no evidence of toxins, food poisoning, or other environmental causes, and again mass hysteria was believed to be the culprit.[3] Finally, in 2002, 10 girls in a rural high school in North Carolina developed epileptic-like seizures and began fainting.[4] After a thorough inspection of the school buildings, nothing was found to explain the outbreak, and it was once again attributed to mass hysteria. It appears that negative emotions and the resulting physical symptoms spread from person to person.

As we discovered with energizers, research suggests that contagious ripples of behavior can quickly spread across a network. That is, energy can travel to one's friends and friends of friends. Indeed, Nicholas Christakis and James Fowler evaluated the impacts of energy diffusion by studying the spreading of happiness from person to person to person and determined that the "three degrees rule" also appears to apply to emotions.[5] Accordingly, they discovered that waves of energy also unfold in clusters. Thus, unhappy people clustered around unhappy people, while happy people clustered around happy people. Their analysis found that individuals are 15 percent more likely to be happy if they are directly connected to another happy person, and this cascading impact continues to two degrees of separation, creating a 10 percent greater likelihood of happiness. That is, if a friend of a friend is happy, a person is 10 percent more likely to be happy, while at three degrees of separation, the effect is 6 percent. Just as with the cases of mass hysteria, energy spreads in clusters.

The contagious nature of our diffusion connections transmits energy in remarkable ways. Energy can quickly spread throughout clusters or entrepreneurial pockets in a network. It therefore stands to reason that if organizations really want to enable agility, they need to begin by following the energy. Indeed, one individual, deep within a network, has the potential to invigorate a groundswell of change, creating the positive energy necessary to affect others within a cluster, engaging people within an entrepreneurial pocket. As Erin Heatherton states, people like to be around those who give off positive energy. In other words, energizers appear to have highly communicable feelings.

Emotional Contagion of Positive Energy

Shortly after Kevin Downey was hired as a lead crisis communicator for DaVita, he was asked to participate in the company's core Academy program. At first he was a little nervous about participating because the event is known for being a bit eccentric. Employees, known as villagers, had notoriously begun singing while donning hats and swords to celebrate at the event, and Downey was a much more low-key, behind-the-scenes kind of guy. By day two, however, Downey was one of the guys dancing in the aisles.[6] Positive energy is contagious at DaVita.

DaVita is a place where ideas flourish. It is indeed a "village," where everyone is able to share and contribute as part of the community, and positive energy flows. Leaders encourage participation in decision making throughout the company, and every six to eight weeks, DaVita holds a "Voice of the Village call" for the whole company to build the art of listening. These Adaptive Space interactions are about sharing ideas, getting feedback, and giving advice on the business. It is also not uncommon to hear the phrase "One for All, and All for One" exclaimed at these gatherings, as the sentiment speaks to the commitment made by all villagers to one another in order to reach their collective goal: "To Be the Greatest Kidney Care Company the World Has Ever Seen." The villagers at DaVita know they can accomplish amazing things together.

These intentional connections seem to be working from a business perspective as well. When CEO Kent Thiry, or the mayor of the village, took over in 1999, the company was on the verge of bankruptcy. Thiry and his leadership team knew they had to do something radical, so they set out on a crazy journey to build a more democratic company where everyone collaborated in making the important decisions.[7] Instead of casting a vision and then cascading it down the hierarchy, leaders invited everyone to lead and share ideas because they knew that villagers were more directly influenced by their relationships than any top-down vision. In fact, even their name, DaVita, was chosen democratically. In 2000, the company was called Total Renal Care. Over a few days, thousands of villagers iterated on new names and voted for DaVita, meaning, "he/she gives life." Since that time, the company's revenues have skyrocketed, and DaVita has flourished on just about every other criterion for success, performing in the top 5 percent of all S&P 500 companies and becoming a stalwart on *Fortune's* Most Admired Companies list.

Perhaps the most impressive part of this story concerns the business DaVita is in. By its very nature, kidney care is a disheartening, emotionally taxing business, and working in a dialysis facility may be one of the hardest jobs there is from this perspective. Patients are chronically ill, and one out of four usually don't survive beyond the first year. Nurses and nursing assistants work long hours and grueling days, and generally for low pay. At times it can feel like an assembly line of patients, and the result for staff is often burnout, depression, and attrition. It is a tough assignment. However, DaVita believes in the power of positive energy, and it has created an environment where people can thrive, thus embodying its name and "giving life."

To truly understand the full and energetic power of DaVita, we need to consider the opposite of positive energy for a moment. Remember the last time you felt totally drained after spending time with a given person. Or a time when you literally felt saturated by negative emotions in your encounter with someone else. Energy vampires are people who seem to suck the very life out of us by zapping any ounce of positive emotion we may have, and sometimes creating an overwhelming sense of anxiety as a result. These negative emotions can spread in an organization much in the same manner as they did with the teenage girls at LeRoy High in the mass hysteria case. Social scientists describe the working factors attributed to this phenomenon as emotional contagions. Just as we may catch a cold by hanging out with someone sick, we can also catch emotions. Furthermore, emotional contagions are often subconscious. When confronted with an energy vampire, we may walk away feeling worse, but we may not have any idea why.

We saw this in action with one organization that was able to study the effects of an individual's energy when joining a new team by surveying new team members as they entered a new group. Interestingly, individuals who joined more negative teams experienced significant energy erosion over the first 18 months of being a part of the team. This decline was three times more significant than any energy losses among individuals who joined positive teams at the same time. Perhaps more important is that this effect began immediately. The moment individuals join a toxic team, they begin to feel its effects.

We are social creatures, and we can be tremendously astute at reading others' social signals, whether consciously or unconsciously. We can do this because our brains operate with an interconnected network of cells known as the mirror neuron system. Subconsciously we are always observing others' facial expressions, body movements, and gestures as an expression of their emotions, and the result is that our own mirror neuron system is activated, causing us to emulate, or mirror, their expressions. This is how we have been taught to relate, or to demonstrate empathy, by letting us feel we have stepped into another's shoes. The problem is, as our own facial muscles mimic those of the other person, our brains go beyond simply placing us in that person's shoes. Rather, our brains, to some extent, literally experience the other's emotions as if they were our own. In short, their negative energy is very contagious.

The good news is that positive energy is also contagious. Even low-key people like Kevin Downey from DaVita can find themselves dancing in the aisle. Ask yourself, when was the last time you were feeling down and your friends lifted you up with their presence and energized you? If organizations want to become agile, they need to go to the edges to get new ideas, and they need to find a friend to bring those ideas to life. Then they need to follow the positive energy to amplify those ideas for greater impact.

Cultivate Contagious Connections

The ability to mirror others' emotions opens social pathways that can influence the diffusion of ideas, insights, and learning across organizations. Optimism can spread rapidly across a network. Social contagions can spiral upward quickly, as we saw with "Crazy Jack" Ma, catapulting positive beliefs and carrying people to a new summit of possibilities, and enabling the diffusion of innovative ideas and bold new concepts. If we follow the positive energy, we can create the social connections necessary to amplify ideas.

Social researcher Jane Dutton has found that these positive energy connections have tremendous benefits.[8] Her research suggests that energy connections, like those at DaVita, lead to improved outcomes and superior decisions. This impact is even greater when it comes to agility, as positive interactions encourage more creativity, greater personal resiliency, and more flexible thinking. Just consider a recent business school experiment.[9] Students were divided into small groups and asked to engage in a simulation in which they were directed to take on the role of department head and advocate for an employee merit increase. Each department head was also part of a "salary committee" that was responsible for allocating a finite set of funds, and their task was to get the most for their own candidate while maximizing the overall benefit to the company. Unannounced to each of them was the fact that each group also had an actor whose only role was to convey one of four different emotions: cheerful enthusiasm, serene warmth, hostile irritability, or depressed sluggishness.

The findings were interesting. Committees in which the actor "spread" positive emotions experienced an increase in positive energy. Surprisingly, the benefits extended beyond the spreading of positive energy. These groups also demonstrated more cooperation, less fighting, and bolder solutions compared with the negative emotion groups. When asked how they accomplished this, the students highlighted such things as superior negotiation strategies and better bargaining techniques. Indeed, they had no inkling that they had caught their group energy from the actor. It is clear that our energy and the energy of those around us spreads, much like the common cold. Yet it is so subtle that we barely notice it. As Dutton's research demonstrates, the benefits aren't so subtle to the organization.

Diffusion connections can also be used to solve problems. On October 29, 2009, the Defense Advanced Research Projects Agency (DARPA) announced a Network Challenge to mark the fortieth anniversary of the Internet.[10] The bizarre and daunting challenge was to locate 10 red weather balloons, placed in undisclosed locations across the entire continent of the United States, a task akin to finding the proverbial needle in a haystack. Or so it seemed.

The balloons were released on December 5, with 4,300 entrants competing for the prize, which was $40,000 to the first person or group that determined all 10 locations. As a last minute entrant, an MIT team, undaunted by the magnitude of the challenge, quickly devised a strategy to contagiously attract people to help find the balloons. The strategy urged individuals to invite interested friends to participate. The team also offered to distribute the prize money amongst the finders of the balloons, along with a smaller reward to those who invited the finders and those who invited the inviters. A website from the MIT team was launched on December 3 to track progress, and each member of the five-person team sent out only one e-mail to an interested friend. Amazingly, in just 48 hours the team enlisted a network of 5,000 people who participated in some cooperative way. Then, on December 5, only 8 hours and 52 minutes into the contest, the team announced that it had located all 10 of the eight-foot-wide balloons!

Unlike the other entrants, who used crowdsourcing or social media, the MIT team created contagious diffusion connections by tapping into the "three degrees of influence rule." They were only interested in high-energy connections, those people who were most likely to be passionate about where the 10 balloons would be, and they correctly hypothesized that they could incentivize friends to be contagious in enlisting support from others who were most interested in finding the balloons. Unlike the other entrants that tried to draw large numbers of people together to crowdsource the challenge, the MIT team pushed interest by incentivizing people to engage others. They focused on finding the contagious energizers.

The Power of Empathy

Another way to generate energy connections is through empathy. As noted, empathy is our ability to understand other people's experiences deeply. It requires us to be able to walk in someone else's shoes, or to suspend our own judgments long enough to be able to see through another person's eyes. Accordingly, it requires the humility to abandon our preconceived ideas and biases, and it necessitates a different level of listening and a deeper understanding. It requires that we have a heightened level of awareness to seek out the wants, needs, and motivations of others. Empathy is a crucial element of human-centered design. The empathy phase of design thinking seeks to develop a deep understanding of users based on their personal experiences and their context. It can also be used to uncover, generate, and amplify energy, such as in the following example.

In October of 2005, Bank of America launched a new product called Keep the Change.[11] The product rounded up purchases made with Bank of America debit cards to the nearest dollar, then transferred the difference, or the "change" to a person's savings account, and Bank of America agreed to match up to $250 a year. Keep the Change was generated from design thinking and empathy. For two months, a cross-functional team of researchers interviewed people from Atlanta, Baltimore, and San Francisco, and they observed people as they paid bills and used their checkbooks. Indeed, they tagged along with mothers as they shopped, visited friends, and made deposits at their bank drive-through, and the result of all these observations was a simple insight. The team had observed one mother in Atlanta who always rounded up her checkbook entries to the nearest dollar. When asked about this, she said that it was easier for her than calculating the change. They then began to see this behavior in their other case observations as well.

A second, more obvious insight was that all of the consumers wanted to save more money but weren't quite sure how to do so. This is where the team of designers went to work. They held nearly 20 brainstorming sessions and generated more than 80 product concepts that aligned to their two core insights. The overwhelming favorite for consumers was rounding up transactions and then transferring the difference to their savings, so the team decided to follow that energy. The product, Keep the Change, was a paradigm shift at the time, reconfiguring current products to address the existing behavior of rounding up. When it was launched, something amazing happened in less than a year. Keep the Change had generated 700,000 new checking accounts and one million new savings accounts. One teller said, "We don't have to even market this product, it sells itself." It appears that people had been waiting for the product, and the power of empathy, which helped to unleash latent energy, made the product possible. Indeed, by more deeply connecting with people's needs, we can create solutions that make such intuitive sense that they practically sell themselves. We are able to follow the energy.

Empathy also has the power to generate the energy necessary to promote diffusion. As we hear individuals' moving stories, we are often compelled to act. This is exactly what happened at GE Healthcare. Doug Dietz is an industrial designer for GE Healthcare who has spent years creating and perfecting the technical capacities of diagnostic imaging equipment (MRI/CT/X-ray).[12] As a great designer, he focused on the details of the enclosures: he designed the system controls and even enhanced the functionality of the displays. In order to do this, Dietz spent a considerable amount of time with the MRI technologist, inquiring about every detail possible to perfect the operation of the machines. Many of these conversations were brutal, as the technologist would frequently tell him, "I struggle with my job, and don't have the time to spend with the families and patients . . . and that is why I got into healthcare in the first place."

One morning that all changed. Dietz was interviewing a technologist when he was asked to leave the MRI room because the next patient was coming in to be scanned. Since he still had more questions for the staff, he decided to wait in the hall. It was there that he first saw his machines from an entirely different perspective, through the eyes of a little girl. Dietz had recently participated in the Stanford d.school bootcamp, where he was taught to empathize with the user, and it was at this moment, in the hall, that he had a revelation. He had always thought of the technologists as the users of his machines, but then he saw a young couple with a weeping little girl walking slowly down the hallway. As they got closer, it was clear that the little girl was terrified. Dietz watched the father lean down and overheard him whisper to his daughter, "Remember, we talked about this, you can be brave."

This hallway experience changed everything for Dietz. All of the sudden, he saw his machine as the little girl saw it, as a big, terrifying box. A plastic brick with a hole in it. The MRI room was of no comfort either, as it was oppressively beige, covered in warning signs, and lit with dim, flickering fluorescent lights. Already frightened, the little girl was asked to lie still on a cold table that slowly moved her into the machine. It was then that things got even worse as the scary machine made horrifying noises, "bang, click, and BANG!" After all of this, the little girl had to be sedated in order to hold still for the exam. When Dietz found out that 80 percent of the children had to be sedated, he was shocked.

From that point forth Dietz could only see the machine through the little girl's eyes. Children clung to their mother's legs, crying, as nurses pried them off and then fed them into the hole of a large, noisy machine, where they were instructed to not move for as long as 40 minutes. This new perspective disturbed Dietz, and he felt compelled to do something. Reminded of his experience at the d.school, he realized that he needed to engage the children to better understand their collective experience. He immediately recruited a few friends to help, engaging four or five designers, not with a logical business case, but with his story. He then set up an interview studio where they could actively engage and interact with the children and their parents. During these exchanges, one child shared a story about how her siblings got to go to camp. Another told them that her brother got trophies all the time. These insights lead Dietz to a novel idea. What if he could create a scanning environment that made the children feel like they were going on an "adventure"?

To do so, Dietz knew that he would have to engage children in the actual design process, so he started building some prototypes and inviting the children into pilot rooms. They experimented with concepts like aromatherapy, calming decorations, and even disco-ball bubbles. Through this process, Dietz and the team discovered that they could use the children's imaginations to their advantage, and the result was the Adventure Series. In one adventure, children are told to get into a canoe, and then instructed to lie down inside. They are then told be really, really still so that they don't rock the boat, and that they might be able to see the fish jumping over them. In the Pirate Adventure, children are placed on a dock amidst decor that shows a shipwreck with some sand castles. The children then enter the CT room on the ship's plank. Finally, there is the Coral City Adventure, which gives children an underwater experience, and the Cozy Camp, where children are scanned in a specialized sleeping bag under a starry sky in an impressive camp setting. In all of these fun scenarios, the fear of the MRI was turned into anticipation and adventure.

As adventure experiences materialized, the business case simultaneously became much clearer. MRI, CT, and x-ray scanners were very expensive and were a limited resource for hospitals, often creating a backlog for appointments. Making this situation even worse was the fact that most young children were so terrified by these machines that they needed to be sedated before a scan. In each of these cases, an anesthesiologist had to be called to administer medication through an intravenous line, causing significant delays and therefore limiting the number of scans each day.

The results of the Adventure Series speak for themselves. Children now enter the room with a sense of excitement, ready for an adventure. The parents now have an adventure aid to proactively provide stories and guide their children through the experience, alleviating some of their own concerns. The technologists, the individuals who struggled with their jobs, have now become amateur actors with adventure scripts. Finally, from the hospital's perspective, sedations have been nearly eliminated, thereby saving on the cost of an anesthesiologist and optimizing the use of an expensive resource by increasing efficiency. In one case, the patient backlog has been reduced from 18 days to zero and patient satisfaction numbers have skyrocketed. By seeing the world through the eyes of a little girl, Dietz was able to catalyze a whole new set of possibilities that would not have otherwise been imagined. He has truly leveraged the power of empathy to create Adaptive Space, helping to alleviate the fears of children while at the same time helping their parents, the technologists, and hospital administrators. Empathy is an enabler for diffusion connections. It generates stories that positively energize the network, with the capacity to spread quickly.

Monitor Present and Potential Energy

In late 2012, Stewart Butterfield and a small team began working on an app that facilitated team collaboration. Midway through the following year, the team was energized from their progress, but they knew that they had a very insular perspective of the product, so they pleaded with and cajoled their friends at other companies to try the product for them. Immediately, the team realized that the product performed quite differently for larger teams. For example, one of the organizations began to use the product for 120 people. Just as with the smaller teams, they could create channels, or chat rooms, for specific topics. However, members of large teams did not intuitively know what was in a given channel. As a result they didn't know which ones to join. The larger organization was clearly not as energized about the product as the design team was, so Butterfield and the team agilely responded with a simple solution. They added fields for a description of a channel, making the product far more intuitive. After adapting the product, the team then progressively recruited larger groups, and once again, it monitored the feedback. From here, the team amplified the features that people were energized about and refined those that were underwhelming. In short, the team created connections to actively monitor the energy.

The product they created is Slack, and the approach that the team used created a billion-dollar company in less than two years.[13] It had also swelled to more than 1.7 million users within that time frame. Perhaps most amazingly, this astonishing growth happened without any major advertising and no sales force. Instead, relying solely on the energy of users, Butterfield and the team actively monitored the energy of users to make Slack very easy to adopt. They realized that they had to tap into the passion of individual users and create a bottoms-up approach in order to bypass the typical corporate terms of service. User by user, companies adopted the product without any formal endorsement. Groundswells of corporate users flocked to the product, quickly winning official backing from companies such as Salesforce, eBay, NASA, and Intuit.

Additionally, by monitoring the energy of its users, Slack decision makers recognized that they had to position the product for local teams, not individuals or organizations. This was the real brilliance in the rapid spread. They tapped into the energy of teams, or clusters in the network. Most apps are sold to individual users. Dropbox, for example, requires an individual to choose whether to download the app and use it, making it purely discretionary to share this fact with friends. Slack was designed differently. It was created to be a team product, and it doesn't benefit an individual who is not part of the team. The trick, then, was to make the product so useful to teams that individuals would be energized to leverage their own social capital to sell it to other team members. The result was exponential diffusion.

The genius of the "Slack attack" was its ability to both monitor the energy and create critical diffusion connections by tapping into the power of energizers. To explore this more deeply, we need to consider how innovation diffuses within a network. Researcher Bryony Reich from the Kellogg School of Management helps to explain this for us. Her research suggests that cohesive networks can either accelerate or dampen idea diffusion.[14] For example, with a messaging app, the majority of contacts must join in for the product to be useful. By their very nature, cohesive groups are insular and therefore limit the entry of innovations. However, if the majority of the people within a cohesive group make a joint decision, diffusion is significantly accelerated. The Slack team's deployment strategy very cleverly dealt with both aspects of this. They quickly generated user passion by monitoring the energy to create simple, intuitive features, and the result was passionate users, or energizers, who were willing to influence their cohesive clusters to adopt the product. Furthermore, as one team within an organization adopted the product, it could echo to other teams. The result was that energizers created the diffusion connections necessary to quickly spread Slack from team to team.

As individuals migrate toward a solution, it can grow into a movement, much like Slack. In one research case an employee called these movements "social snowballs." They start out small and are barely identifiable when compared to all the other activities. However, once they build a little momentum they start rolling downhill, growing in size and magnitude. Finally, they become so big they are impossible to ignore. The trick, then, is to find them before they become too large. When it comes to Adaptive Space, energy is everything, and great innovators know how to monitor it, leverage it, and follow it.

There is another reason why organizations need to continually monitor energy. Organizations tend to settle into zombie projects—that is, projects doomed for failure that are kept on life support much longer than they should be, sucking up resources and limiting growth investments elsewhere, stifling agility. Some ideas are just bad, de-energizing, or perhaps simply outdated and need to be modified or decommissioned. As a result, the level of energy around a given solution needs to be constantly evaluated. Internal entrepreneurs need to pulse check their ideas regularly and respond accordingly.

This is exactly what happened with the evolution of Twitter. In early 2006, Odeo was a San Francisco–based company that focused on podcast aggregation and search. The organization's website enabled users to create, record, and share podcasts with a simple Adobe Flash–based interface. The members of the board realized that they were not energized about the future, however, and so they staged an event to reenergize themselves. This event was a daylong hacking session where individuals broke up into teams to tear apart existing concepts and share their best ideas for the future.

While enjoying some Mexican food and sitting on a children's slide in a park, one Odeo engineer, Jack Dorsey, shared a simple way to use text messages to send status updates to small groups with his teammates. Within two weeks of this challenge, Dorsey and his colleague, Biz Stone, had created the first Twitter prototype. Dorsey's first "use case" for the concept was broadcasting to a group of people that a club was "happening" through a single text message to all of his friends. The prototype was received well, but it needed a name. The duo wanted something that related to a phone vibrating in a person's pocket, something akin to a twitch. From there, Stone thought about how a bird tweets and suggested Twitter. In July of 2006, they then launched a full-scale version of Twitter. Today, tweets connect pop stars to politicians plus millions of ordinary folks, and it all happened because employees and the board were not energized about Odeo.

Energy is essential to agility. If people are fired up about something they are far more likely to do whatever is necessary to bring it to life. Conversely, when they aren't energized, there is little hope for success. Organizations need to constantly monitor energy. They also need to create diffusion connections to amplify positive energy and shift interactions when energy is low.

High-Energy Connections

In 2009, Airbnb was in significant trouble.[15] The company had launched as just another bed and breakfast start-up, in its founders' loft in San Francisco, and like many challenged start-ups, it had tried many ideas with little early success. At its lowest point, revenues had plummeted to just $200 per week and the founders had maxed out their individual credit cards. They knew that they had to do something quickly, or Airbnb would be out of business.

Then the team noticed something. After poring over their search results for their New York City listings, they discovered a pattern: all the photos were terrible. People were using their camera phones to post their listings and poor photographic quality was noticeable, so the team did something radical: they spent their remaining resources to travel to New York. Once there, they rented a camera and spent some time with their customers. They upgraded all the amateur photos to beautiful high-resolution pictures, and their revenue began to increase immediately.

This was the turning point for Airbnb in another way. The technology-oriented founders recognized that they couldn't code their way out of trouble. To be successful, they had to create high-energy connections directly with their customers. Today, new employees are therefore taught from the beginning to go out, meet customers, and come up with real-world solutions for what customers want. Airbnb has thus created Adaptive Space to ensure high-energy connections with its customers. New hires engage in a field visit during their first or second week, where they interact with customers, engage in their struggles, and share their experiences with other employees. The results are contagious, high-energy connections with customers that ripple positively throughout Airbnb.

When it comes to networks, we always assume "more is better." However, this is not always the case. Sometimes, better is better. That is, we need to create high-energy connections and networks that are actively engaged in the issues. Airbnb did just this. It was able to empathically connect with its customer to provide a unique service that engages customers. The question therefore becomes, how do organizations tap into the power of these high-energy connections to enable Adaptive Space? This is the question that General Motors asked and answered with its Cadillac division.

In 2015, a small team of cross-functional leaders within GM was challenged to reimagine the luxury experience for the next generation of consumers. The team represented individuals from such areas as marketing, technology, operations, quality, and manufacturing. They began their journey inter-viewing customers in luxury retail at places such as the Domain upscale shopping center in Austin and in high-end hotels like the JW Marriott, also in Austin, and the Four Seasons, in New York. As a result of these interviews, the team recognized that exclusivity of access and privileges is central to the luxury expe-rience. After testing a multitude of prototypes in the field, the team also realized that the emerging generation preferred access verses ownership. Armed with these insights, the team set out to eliminate the hassle associated with car ownership by creat-ing BOOK by Cadillac. BOOK is a subscription service that provides on-demand access to an entire collection of Cadillac vehicles. However, this is only the beginning of the story.

For years, Cadillac had been a pioneer in selling luxury vehicles. The organization had zero experience in running a sub-scription service. Changing the business model of a century-old company was a daring move indeed. Lead by Melody Lee from Cadillac Marketing, the team decided to engage a small group of influencers to cocreate the subscription service. They invited 20 influencers, including some skeptics, to build the service. For three months they collected insights and feedback from these high-energy connections using a combination of photo journals and workshops. Together, they listened to issues, they explored possibilities, and they generated an assortment of ideas.

By following the energy of these connections, Lee and the team were able to create a service that aligns with the needs of a demand economy, on the customer's terms. In short, the influencers wanted a "simpler way to get behind the wheel." Accordingly, the service was designed to remove the pain of ownership by covering the insurance premiums, taxes, and maintenance fees with no long-term commitments. The service also provides a concierge to manage the delivery experience and to handle any issues while driving. Finally, the team designed an intuitive app that enables subscribers to request a vehicle, schedule a delivery, and then exchange it when needed. In the end, Cadillac aimed to follow the energy and provide a simple, flexible, and personal solution to reimagine the luxury experience for the next generation of consumers, and it appears the company succeeded.

The initial response has been overwhelmingly positive. While the company limited the first market beta launch to only 50 customers in Manhattan, it received over 8,000 applications. The media also seemed to be interested in the service, with more than 200 initial news articles and over 89 million earned media impressions.

Organizations like DaVita, Slack, and Airbnb have figured out how to follow the energy. They generate positive energy and create the social connections necessary to amplify ideas. They enable the diffusion of innovative ideas and bold new concepts, and they create the connections necessary to follow and amplify the energy. Last, they create Adaptive Space by leveraging energizers.

There are five core strategies for following the energy and creating diffusion connections:

1. **Create a village.** Organizations need to create a community where everyone can contribute and share. Much like DaVita, leaders need to listen and engage the voice of the village and create an environment for positive energy.

2. **Engage in empathy.** Organizations need to tap into the power of empathy to more deeply understand users' needs

and unleash latent energy. They can do this through the discovery and development of stories that positively energize the network and spread quickly.

3. **Create a "Slack attack."** Organizations need to both monitor the energy and create critical diffusion connections by tapping into the power of energizers. They must pay attention to the energy of users and adjust accordingly.

4. **Kill zombie projects.** Organizations tend to invest in projects that are doomed for failure. They must be willing to modify or actively decommission such projects and shift investments to high-energy bets, as Twitter did.

5. **Find social snowballs.** Organizations must pay better attention to the small activities that have the potential to grow. They need to constantly monitor momentum in order to arrest and then leverage it.

9

• ———————————— •

Embrace the Conflict

*For good ideas and true innovation, you need
human interaction, conflict, argument, and debate.*

—MARGARET HEFFERNAN

On December 21, 1937, the world's first full-length animated feature film, produced in Technicolor, premiered at
the Radio City Music Hall in Los Angeles. At its conclusion, Walt Disney waited for what seemed like an eternity, as
the star-studded crowd momentarily remained silent. Then, in
a roaring outburst, the crowd leaped to its feet and erupted into
a standing ovation. The audience was emotionally stirred, with
many fighting back tears, for they had just witnessed brilliance.
In his review of the movie, Frank Nugent wrote, "Sheer fantasy,
delightful, gay, and altogether captivating, touched the screen
yesterday when Walt Disney's long-awaited feature-length cartoon of the Grimm fairy tale, *Snow White and the Seven Dwarfs*,
had its local [showing]. Let your fears be quieted at once: Mr.

Disney and his amazing technical crew have outdone themselves."[1] The film went on to become a major box-office smash hit, earning nearly $8 million during its original running, which was a staggering sum of money in the midst of the Great Depression, and more than any other motion picture of its time. Indeed, the movie's lifetime gross has been estimated to exceed $400 million over the years since its initial release, and some have proclaimed the feature to be the greatest movie ever made.

These are stunning proclamations when you consider the fact that Walt's decision to make the world's first animated feature was wildly criticized at the time. Literally up until the day of the premiere of *Snow White and the Seven Dwarfs*, the project was dubbed "Disney's folly." The very thought of an animated film flew in the face of popular wisdom at the time.[2] Prior to *Snow White*, animation was widely dismissed as suitable only for children's cartoons. Walt himself had inadvertently contributed to this perception with the raving success of his main character, Mickey Mouse, who was portrayed though crudely drawn short clips designed to entertain children. Walt had another vision, however. He believed that animation could be presented as an emotional feature film that captivated all audiences. Naysayers included even those closest to Walt. His wife, Lillian, warned him that audiences, especially adults, wouldn't sit through a feature-length cartoon fantasy about dwarfs, and it didn't stop there. Walt's brother Roy, who managed the company's finances, was outraged by the expenditures for the movie, which were nearly eight times the original estimate of $250,000. Roy knew that anything less than a raging success would bankrupt the studio.

Walt however, charged forward in spite of the dissent. His passion was to make the film both technically superb and enchanting. He knew that to overcome conventional wisdom, he had to create a film with dramatic characters that ensured audiences would experience deeper emotional connections than they had to any previous animations. To do so, he needed his animators to act more dramatically than ever before. Focusing on creating disruptive connections with his team, Walt forged a united passion that compelled them to believe that they could accomplish something that no one else had ever believed was possible.

On one winter night in 1934, Walt instructed the team to meet him at the Disney soundstage. When they arrived in suspense, Walt was standing alone in the spotlight, on a dark stage, where, for the next several hours, he single-handedly acted out the story of Snow White.[3] He wanted his team to experience the depth of emotions he envisioned. He personally acted out each character, channeling their voices, embodying the chilling tones of the wicked queen as she spoke to each of the seven dwarves. Walt knew that if he were going to do something remarkable, he would first have to disrupt his own team, so he used what he knew best, story. His passion for the film won over his team as he captivated their emotions, and together they charged ahead with his vision.

Enabling his team to connect emotionally with his vision was only the beginning of an ongoing series of challenges. In the early animation sequences, Snow White's movements were very jerky. Walt created more disruptive connections by bringing in ballet dancers and having his animators study their motions and then challenging them to draw their naturally fluid movements with all-encompassing precision. The Seven Dwarfs were an even greater challenge. He knew they each had to have an individual personality; seven identical characters running around would bore the audience. That individuality required excruciating levels of detail. The team would sometimes take an entire day debating a single close-up for a given dwarf, whereby each name was altered countless times, with some prototypes being Dizzy, Lazy, Stuffy, and Burpy. In the end, the studio spent four years developing seven engaging personalities. Walt was maniacal, and nothing was going to stop him. The result was an epic movie that shattered conventional wisdom in every way imaginable, tapping into the world's imagination at an entirely new level and opening up a whole new set of possibilities.

Walt created the disruptive connections necessary to enable his team to charge forward against conventional wisdom, by acting both as a challenger and a connector; first, by envisioning a new possibility, and then by uniting his team with a compelling passion. Walt knew that he had to prepare his team in advance for the onslaught of external controversy and criticism, and he also knew that there would be many internal disagreements. As author and entrepreneur Margaret Heffernan once said, "For good ideas and true innovation, you need human interaction, conflict, argument, and debate." Innovation is a social phenomenon, and for ideas to advance, they need to combine, collide, and evolve over time. The development of *Snow White* is one illustration of this phenomenon, exemplified primarily by its tremendous agility. Indeed, the characters, plot, and effects all changed repeatedly throughout the exertions of artistic creation. The team not only released the world's first animated feature film, its members also had to invent the processes to reach their goal, shattering conventional wisdom along the way.

Walt knew that the main attraction of the story was the Seven Dwarfs. Therefore, he challenged his team to create more possibilities for "screwiness" and "gags" in association with them, and he discovered that provoking his team seemed to work. Just consider the most beloved of the seven, Dopey. He exemplifies "screwiness" as an innocent, beardless dwarf with a puppy dog–like personality. Dopey is portrayed as constantly out of sync with the others and doomed to carry the red tail light, all without uttering a single word. The audience loved him. Walt knew he had to keep pushing his team to bring the dwarfs to life. At one point he even sent a memo offering five dollars for any dwarf "gags" that made it into the film to make the audience experience more interesting, such as the scene where the dwarfs' noses pop up at the foot of Snow White's bed. Walt was simply phenomenal at challenging his team. He knew that they had to debate ideas and create new possibilities, but most important, he knew they had to do this together.

The Uplift of Conflict

Conflict is essential to advancing ideas because the resistance to new ideas generates a pressure-testing effect, enhancing and ultimately creating better organizational fit. In other words, as ideas and concepts are modified in response to conflict, they are far more likely to be endorsed. Furthermore, the initial resistance creates organizational lift—much the way headwinds assist with an aircraft's takeoff. This phenomenon appears counterintuitive, as one would think that as an aircraft took off, it would be the wind pushing it from behind that would give it an extra boost rather than the wind pushing against it. Yet accelerating into a gale of wind creates a "wheels up" effect even faster. For example, a Boeing 747 needs to reach 180 mph of airspeed before it can become airborne. Yet, if the same aircraft is charging into a

30 mph headwind, it only needs to accelerate to 150 mph. The velocity of air passing over the wings pulls the plane upward. The same can be true for ideas inside organizations. By charging into the headwinds of conflict, an idea can reach "wheels up" faster.

While takeoff is a dangerous phase in aviation, some ill-fated outcomes actually benefit organizations. Failing faster isn't conventional wisdom. Yet, this is exactly what McDonald's has learned to do. The company has figured out that time-to-market impact is condensed when it fails sooner. Just consider the Snack Wrap story as a case in point.[4] McDonald's needed to create a new chicken item that would appeal to drive-through customers, so it quickly tried almost 100 different concepts, rapidly weeding out the ones that were too complicated or that simply missed the mark. The company began beta testing the more promising ideas with consumers, with many of them failing fairly quickly. Nevertheless, it was able to get to the current version of the Snack Wrap more rapidly as a result of this strategy. In all, the product was developed and scaled to mass market in a mere six months, an astonishingly short period of time given McDonald's size and complexity. The company has created a discipline out of failing faster in order to succeed sooner. This isn't conventional wisdom, but it leads to the "wheels up" faster phenomenon.

The Power of Passionate Dissent

Conflict is also important for another reason. The absence of conflict usually means there is an absence of passion. The fact is that most people simply aren't willing to push for things they don't believe in. Therefore conflict serves as an antecedent to agility. Argument and debate are essential to generating the creative destruction of the current operational system and ushering in new possibilities. Just think about it: a breakthrough requires something to break through, thus creating conflict, and behind every major breakthrough is a fierce conviction, or passion.

Lipitor is a breakthrough cholesterol-lowering medicine that almost wasn't. Early in the development process, the drug was internally viewed as just another statin in an already crowded field. Powerhouse pharmaceutical companies like Merck, Bristol-Myers, and Novartis were far ahead with their own statin drugs and the marketing executives projected that Lipitor sales might approach $300 million a year at best, which was a mere fraction of the market. During the review, one marketer even went to far as to say, "I wish someday you guys could make us a drug we could sell." Roger Newton, the so-called "father of Lipitor," had a very different perspective, however.[5] He was passionate about the possibilities of the drug and believed it was superior to the other drugs in the space. Nevertheless, every rational argument he made fell on deaf ears. Left with no other alternative, he pleaded for a clinical evaluation. He persuaded Pfizer to fund the initial round of testing on a couple of dozen volunteers.

As Newton suggested, subsequent testing proved Lipitor to be superior to all other statin drugs, with the testing even surpassing his own expectations. The drug quickly earned the nickname "turbostatin" in the marketplace, and the rest is history. At its peak, the drug provided nearly one-quarter of Pfizer's annual revenue, becoming the most commercially successful drug of all time. Newton's persistence and passion not only saved the drug from being discarded but also propelled its ascension. It certainly wasn't without conflict, however, as being a challenger isn't for the faint of heart. Driven by a fierce passion that they are doing what is best for the future of the organization, challengers press, push, and argue their way toward new possibilities.

Peter Kosak, an engineer at GM, is this type of challenger. He had an idea and asked what if GM could create convenient on-demand automotive access and a multimodal transportation platform for urban environments? Indeed, urban mobility has grown into a real problem. City congestion restricts driving, parking limitations are problematic, and overall, auto ownership is very expensive. Kosak's idea was to create a mobility platform that leveraged a broad set of interconnected solutions ranging from electric bikes, to cars, to mass transit. The problem was that GM sold cars. To many, car sharing and a multimodal approach meant likely selling fewer cars, thereby generating significant internal resistance.

Carving a new path toward a breakthrough within a current business model is never easy. However, as one person noted, "Peter's the rare combination of a visionary and gladiator." Indeed, as an executive engineer, Kosak knew that the best way to get buy-in was to get started, so that is what he did. Kosak leveraged his informal network to connect a small band of cross-functional innovators. Together, they embraced the conflict, testing, tweaking, and iterating in response to criticism. They decided to start small by creating a remote access app that enabled vehicle control, and then to run a small pilot composed of an employee experiment with GM-owned vehicles. While the cynics actively opposed this pilot, the ragtag team of passionate innovators was able to garner some organizational momentum with participating employees.

Ultimately, Kosak and his band of innovators created the foundation for what is now referred to as Maven, a car-sharing platform that provides on-demand vehicle access. It is a mobility platform designed for the true urbanite who has no desire to own a car, yet occasionally has the need to have access to a vehicle. In the first year of operations alone, Maven members accumulated more than 80 million miles and expanded to 17 cities including Atlanta, Chicago, Los Angeles, and New York. The very name, Maven, is representative of trailblazers creating a new path, and that is exactly what Kosak and his team have done.

It might be easy to look at people like Roger Newton and Peter Kosak as heroic gladiators who passionately pleaded or fought in response to the conflict from the operational system. However, when you look deeper, they were actually challengers who banded together with other passionate innovators, creating disruption connections and charging into the resulting conflict.

Designing in Dissent

As we discovered from Solomon Asch's work in Chapter 7, there is a strong tendency for individuals to lean toward social conformity. Participants in his experiment repeatedly selected an "obviously erroneous" answer when others did. However, what we did not discuss was how Asch also found that participants didn't conform nearly as often if they had even a single "ally."[6] That is, when a single person (a nonconformist in the experiment) gives the correct answer and everyone else provides an erroneous one, an individual is far more likely to go against the larger group and select the one he or she believes to be accurate. In other words, a single nonconformist, or ally, significantly increases the chances of an individual choosing his or her true personal belief. A nonconformist ally appears to give people permission to dissent from the broader group or organization.

In her TED Talk "Dare to Disagree," Margaret Heffernan tells a tremendous story about the conflict that Dr. Alice Stewart endured.[7] Dr. Stewart, a member of the social medicine department at Oxford, was concerned about the growing incidence of childhood cancer in the 1950s. In particular, she was interested in finding out why many of these cases were from children of affluence as opposed to poverty, with the latter generally being correlated more strongly with disease. Therefore, she conducted a comprehensive study to evaluate these cases, and her findings were very surprising: children of mothers who had had an x-ray during pregnancy were almost twice as likely to have cancer as children of mothers who had not.

Understandably, Dr. Stewart's findings were met with outrage.[8] Most physicians were convinced that there was no danger in the low dose of radiation emitted from an x-ray, and they were backed up by the entire nuclear industry. Dr. Stewart knew she had to be certain of her results, so she partnered with a statistician named George Kneale. Kneale's job was quite simple: prove Dr. Stewart wrong. Accordingly, Kneale actively pursued a dissenting view. He crunched the data in every way possible to construct a counterargument, and yet in the end, Kneale provided Dr. Stewart with the statistical support and confidence needed to charge into the conflict. It took nearly 20 years, but other scientists replicated her findings and prenatal x-rays were finally ceased.

Few people have the courage to charge into the conflict and risk their reputations and face alienation from their professional peers, as Dr. Stewart did. Serving as the lone nonconformist, her passion to solve a very disturbing problem was much greater than her desire to be right. Accordingly, she knew that she had to intentionally design dissent into the back-and-forth challenges from Kneale and relentlessly pursue an unbiased outcome. She understood that the only way she could verify the truth was to be challenged from every angle possible, and this level of debate served to help solidify her original position. It should be noted that this conflict could just as easily have opened her eyes to different perspectives. Indeed, challengers like Dr. Stewart know that they need to charge into the conflict and face all possible perspectives in order to build an inner confidence around their argument.

Alice Stewart was able to be the lone nonconformist because she designed dissent into her research. Her passion to find the cause of these childhood cancers superseded her need to conform. She was willing to charge into this conflict, but she needed to be confident. George Kneale provided this through designed dissent. Together they relentlessly pursued an unbiased outcome. Ultimately, this tenacity made it possible for others to be nonconformist. Stewart was the ally that made it all right for others to finally lean away from the social conformity of their profession.

Challengers aren't afraid of dissent. They know that it is a necessary ingredient for creative destruction. Without dissention, we all have the tendency to follow the group, and we can become like lemmings, mindlessly joining in with a group, even if we are rushing head-on into destruction.

Enabling Give-and-Take

This is the magic of Pixar. The company rarely tries to do the same thing twice and each movie is a new creation with many different ideas. Furthermore, Pixar knows that initial ideas are what they call "ugly babies." All new ideas begin somewhat awkwardly, being incomplete and fragile.[9] They are also vulnerable, as are their creators. Pixar thus recognizes that every movie begins with ill-defined concepts. The filmmakers are therefore highly disciplined at iterating these ideas to make them better. For their creators, this is a humbling act. The first version of the movie *Up*, for example, included a king in a castle in the clouds. However, the creative team heavily scrutinized and refined this initial version until they had thrown out everything except one bird. The film went through countless iterations, each time inching closer to a final story, with Pixar understanding the need to endure many failures in order to produce a brilliant final product. Creators know that this is a give-and-take kind of process and some of their ideas will not make it beyond infancy. Others, however, are beautified into marvelous creations. Indeed creators recognize that it is better to charge into the conflict sooner, with colleagues, rather than later, with an audience.

Leaders set the tone by modeling these practices, and it seems to be infectious as similar practices are being employed throughout Pixar. Everyone has the freedom to communicate with everyone else, and some groups even choose to hold "dailies," in which people share incomplete work with one another, because it is a safe environment for everyone to offer and challenge ideas. Not surprisingly, the debate seems to make everyone more creative. Indeed, Pixar decision makers believe that good ideas emerge from interaction, conflict, and debate. They encourage dissent.

Pixar also knows that this requires an environment of mutual respect and trust. Accordingly, the company leaders are intent on building healthy social dynamics. They know that an idea isn't just an idea, but it also represents the person who creates it. When you make a judgment about an idea, you are also judging its creator. So Pixar creates an environment that is tough on ideas, but respectful to creators. Treating ideas as ugly babies that need to be nurtured into maturity, the company facilitates give-and-take. It seems to be working; Pixar has built an incredible track record and continues to deliver breakthrough movies.

Unfortunately, not all organizations have been afforded the opportunity to build cohesive cultures as Pixar has. Nor can most organizations wait passively for challengers to rise up. Instead, they need to enable Adaptive Space to ensure there is enough local conflict to generate creative tension, but not so much that it thwarts the grander purpose. This is exactly what Quicken Loans does.[10] The company has developed a work ethos that has turned a classically dull and grueling mortgage origination business into a dynamic, creative environment, and it doesn't shy away from conflict. People are taught to fight against conventional wisdom and push boundaries as they are challenged to "find a better way." The company's billionaire founder, Dan Gilbert, epitomizes the role of being a challenger: his core business was the result of shattering conventional wisdom. In the 1980s he became interested in the mortgage business and started Rock Financial, which evolved into a solid regional business. Gilbert, however, wasn't satisfied with solid.

In 1998 he made a bold move, sending an e-mail to his staff, suggesting that someone would eventually utilize the Internet to transform the mortgage business. He knew this was a huge opportunity, so he committed the resources necessary to "get this true revolution going." He then went on to say to his team, "Let's change the mortgage world forever." Gilbert backed up this challenge by assigning a small group of the company's smartest minds to create a website capable of handling mortgages in all 50 states from one central office. Within a year, Rockloans.com was launched. The business was later renamed

Quicken Loans, and today it operates as one of the nation's largest mortgage lenders.

Gilbert has embedded this type of work ethos in what he and the company call the ISMs, a set of snappy principles that are self-explanatory. Newcomers are challenged to bring the ISMs to life through a daylong indoctrination session, led by Gilbert himself. They include ideologies such as "ignore the noise," "simplicity is genius," and "every second counts," and they operate as mission-driven principles that keep people focused on things beyond local success. Perhaps this is best represented by the ISM "We are the 'they,'" which states, "There is no 'they.' We are the 'they.' One team. United. All in the mission together. No corporate barriers. No boundaries. Just open doors, open minds and an open culture rooted in trust."[11]

Quicken has grown into a mortgage empire, but it continues to fight for a small company feel.[12] This is illustrated through what's called Bullet Time. Every Monday afternoon, members of the IT staff get together for four hours to work on projects of their own choosing. Bullet Time serves as a rapid-fire give-and-take exchange of ideas, designed to break down boundaries and create something for the grander mission, and it seems to be working. The company has been a stalwart at the top of the J.D. Power list of companies highest in customer satisfaction among mortgage originators, while also continually making *Fortune*'s "100 Best Companies to Work For" list.

Mission Thwarts Conflict

In the summer of 1954, a group of young boys were invited to participate in a summer camp in the Sans Bois Mountains in southeastern Oklahoma. When they arrived, half of the boys were directed to one cabin, while the other half went to a different cabin. Each cabin had its own separate swimming, boating, and camping areas. The two groups of boys were very much alike, having been intentionally selected to be of similar height and musculature, with many of the same interests. The other thing they had in common was that neither group knew they were part of a social experiment.

More specifically, the boys were participating in one of the most famous studies in social psychology history, the Sherif's Robbers Cave experiment.[13] The study was devised by Turkish-American social psychologist Muzafer Sherif, who was interested in intergroup conflict, and it was carried out across three phases. In the first of these phases, the boys were encouraged to connect and bond in isolation from the other group through participation in typical camp activities. Interestingly, within the first seven days, the two camps had each constructed a set of clear, informal norms. They had established informal leaders and rules, and even group status had been clearly established, with the high- and low-status boys each delineated. The clusters had also selected group names, the Rattlers and the Eagles. Near the end of phase one, the groups were introduced, whereupon they immediately began to refer to each other as "outsiders" or "intruders."

During phase two, the Rattlers and the Eagles engaged in a series of direct competitions, such as baseball, tug-of-war, touch football, and tent pitching, to name a few. Then, they participated in a high-stakes scavenger hunt group competition, where counselors offered rewards and trophies, and the conflict between the two groups quickly intensified. The Eagles burned the Rattlers' flag, and the Rattlers retaliated with a nighttime raid on the

Eagles' cabin, where they flipped over beds, ripped the mosquito net, and even went as far as stealing a stack of comic books. The Eagles were infuriated, upping the ante with a full-out counterattack in the dining hall where they had come armed with bats and socks filled with stones to use as weapons. At this point the counselors quickly intervened to prevent the actual assault from occurring. However, it had become very clear that noticeable boundaries had been drawn and all of the boys were strongly identifying themselves as either Rattlers or Eagles.

Conflict between the two groups was intense, and it was at this point that phase three was begun. Phase three was designed for reconciliation. In a cease-fire mode, the two groups were pulled together to interact on an equal footing during movies, joint meals, and other activities, but the effort seemed futile, as the Rattlers and the Eagles refused to associate with each other. Indeed, at one point, the two groups even resorted to throwing food at each other. Next, the researchers moved to another strategy where they created common, superordinate goals—that is, objectives larger than either of the two groups. For example, the camp's drinking water had been intentionally clogged, and the counselors strategically pulled all the boys together to help solve the problem. The two groups hastily began to work together to unplug the water, but once they had accomplished the task, intergroup conflict continued, although not at the same level of intensity. Next the boys were asked to work together to help with a stalled food truck, and so on. After each successive superordinate mission, the level of antagonism between the Rattlers and the Eagles was diminished even further, until it fully dissipated by the end of the camp experience. During the closing ceremony, the Rattlers even splurged, spending $5 to buy malts for the Eagles.

We could dismiss Sherif's experiment as typical 11-year-old boy behavior, except that the same dynamics take place in organizations every day. "Us" verses "them" interactions are as prevalent with working adults as they are with 11-year-olds, and unfortunately, this type of intergroup behavior is rarely positive for agility. It stifles progress, as the focus turns inward and toward the other group and distracts the company from the external pressures. This is why challengers and brokers are so crucial. Challengers help to set a superordinate mission, propelling cohesive clusters beyond their local interests and group identities. Organizations that can keep focus on missional goals can quickly work past the intergroup conflict. This is the magic of Pixar: its innovators and creators are able to embrace the conflict that emerges at the individual creator, or group, level because they are focused on the superordinate mission of another phenomenal breakthrough movie. The local give-and-take interactions are thus viewed as part of the grander creative process. This was also how Walt Disney compelled his team of animators to produce sheer brilliance with *Snow White and the Seven Dwarfs*. He elicited local conflict and debate to stimulate passionate creativity that focused on the grander story.

Brokers, on the other hand, are critical to ensure that the boundaries of the local clusters or entrepreneurial pockets don't become so rigid that they lose sight of the grander purpose. They provide the bridges necessary for exchanges and conflicts to be constructive. Brokers reduce the insularity between the Rattlers and the Eagles of organizations, embodying the Quicken Loan's ISM of "We are the 'they,'" or perhaps operating as the incoming CFO of Pixar did. Remember from Chapter 2, Lawrence Levy was able to navigate the conflict between the two camps of Steve Jobs and Pixar's senior executives and refocus them on the superordinate mission of the launching of *Toy Story*. Indeed, both challengers and brokers serve to elicit conflict to propel the grander purpose, or a superordinate challenge, creating an updraft for greater lift and opening up Adaptive Space.

Diversity at the Core

Intergroup biases aren't limited to working teams, as the study conducted by social researchers Paul Ingram and Michael Morris suggests.[14] In this study, the question posed was how people would interact in an informal networking event. In an attempt to answer this question, Ingram and Morris decided to hold a casual social where executive MBA participants could gather to mingle over hors d'oeuvres, wine, and beer. In all, about 100 people participated, including managers, entrepreneurs, consultants, and bankers. Prior to the event, participants were asked to identify those individuals that they already knew, and it was determined that on average, people already knew about one-third of the group. They were also asked why they planned to attend the event, and 95 percent of them said to "meet new people." Only a few people suggested they would attend to deepen existing relationships.

Ingram and Morris tracked the interactions during the event and quickly discovered that in spite of individuals' intentions, their behaviors proved to be quite different. On average each guest had 14 interactions during the evening, with previous acquaintances accounting for a disproportionately large number of these interactions. This led researchers to believe that we are simply more comfortable hanging out with people we already know, even when that isn't our original intent. Indeed, this isn't just about a previous acquaintance. As social creatures, we are prone to the tendency of homophily, whereby we are simply more attracted to individuals who are similar to us. The problem is that this tendency can create insularity like that of the Rattlers and the Eagles.

Diversity is critical to organizational agility. Indeed we now know that a diverse environment produces better outcomes and varied experiences offer a wider set of perspectives, and research continues to prove that this is true. McKinsey has been studying diversity in the workplace for years. It found that organizations that are in the top quartile for gender and ethnic diversity consistently produce financial returns above the industry medians.[15] Conversely, firms in the bottom quartile in diversity are statistically less likely to perform with above-average returns. The bottom line is that diversity matters. However, the network structure of diversity is equally important. For example, the effects of homophily can limit the impact of diversity. As we have just seen, if people are limiting interactions to the people they already know or those most like them, they can't benefit from diversity. For diversity to enhance agility, organizations need to maintain open networks where everyone can actively feel comfortable interacting with everyone else.

Consider the research case where we mapped out a network of 500 individuals within a large service organization that had demonstrated agility. Nearly 44 percent of individuals in the network were women (as represented by the dark nodes in Figure 9.1). However, it is their position in the network that made them agile. While there is clearly homophily in the network, with women clustering with other women and men clustering with other men (as represented by the grey nodes in Figure 9.1), there is also diversity at the core. That is, the center of the network has a nice mixture of gender diversity, ensuring that more diverse perspectives are being more widely distributed. This is the type of diversity that drives agility.

FIGURE 9.1 Gender Diversity in a Service Organization

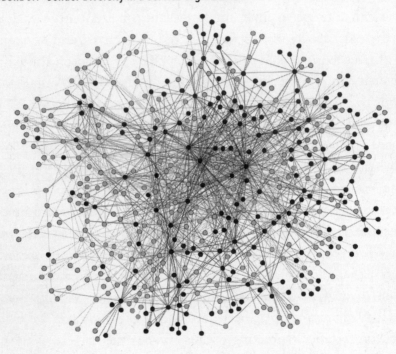

Many diversity and inclusion strategies have the unintended consequence of generating greater cohesion within similar members of a diverse group. That is, they deepen relationships in the same manner as the Rattlers and the Eagles. As we learned, this can result in unhealthy intragroup conflict. A much better way to do this is to challenge multi-diverse groups to focus on superordinate goals or a grander mission.

Consider the case where a large financial service company was having difficulty satisfying internal employees with its benefit services. The company had adopted a "one size fits all" model to drive optimization, and while many employees really liked the new approach, many others were highly dissatisfied. The organization therefore decided to use a unique approach to solving this problem. It brought together a highly diverse group of men and women and challenged them to design a better solution. In the end, the group was able to maintain the efficiencies of the first solution yet provide the variations necessary for people of different languages, life stages, and income brackets. Satisfaction went up for all groups.

Of course there are other types of diversity that are also critical to agility. W.L. Gore and Associates ensures that people from multiple locations, functions, and levels are pulled into the core for critical decisions. The company is a great illustration of an organization that embraces superordinate goals. Associates are given much freedom to dabble with new ideas and then to openly socialize them across their personal lattice, or network. However, they ultimately need to demonstrate that the product opportunity is real. At the post-dabble juncture, cross-functional groups are therefore formed to conduct a "Real, Win, Worth" review. Associates first want to challenge the opportunity by ensuring that there is a potential for "Real" impact. They then objectively evaluate the possibility for Gore to be able to "Win" in the market with the assets that it currently has, and finally, they challenge the individual to ensure that the outcomes are "Worth" the efforts associated with winning.

The intent of these peer reviews is to bring diversity into the core, pulling people together from varying backgrounds and experiences to scrutinize ideas and ensure that they can win in the marketplace and make a profit for the company. In response to the scrutiny, the associate is therefore challenged to experiment and learn with low-risk solutions. The result for Gore has been a multitude of innovative products and solutions that have been stretched beyond their original concept, therefore, enhancing agility.

This process can take some time. For example, Glide dental floss took many years to become a success. Gore executives knew it was a real product, but they just couldn't figure out how to get it into the market. Then John Spencer had an idea. He started promoting the floss directly to the dentists. Spencer handed out free samples of the floss to them and they were impressed. Sales finally took off, generating $45 million in sales before it was sold to Procter & Gamble in 2003.[16] In fact, many companies would have given up on the product, but not Gore. Gore chose to morph, adapt, and adjust to find a way forward. One of the reasons the company is so agile is because it pulls functional diversity into the core.

Organizations like Pixar, Quicken Loans, and W.L. Gore and Associates have figured out how to charge into the conflict. They enhance agility through interaction, argument, and debate, and they create disruptive connections in order to do so. There are five core strategies for charging into the conflict:

1. **Focus on wheels up.** Organizations need to charge into the headwinds of conflict to create better uplift. They need to create velocity to accelerate time-to-impact, as McDonalds does.
2. **Encourage mavens.** Organizations need to find and support the trailblazers to create new paths. Adaptive Space must be created for challengers to follow their

convictions, and mavens must be encouraged to band together.

3. **Create allies of dissent.** Organizations need to provide permission for nonconformists to dissent. Confidence must be built to charge into the conflict, and dissent must be intentionally designed into exchanges.

4. **Support "We are the 'they.'"** Organizations must ensure that they focus on building one united team, as Quicken Loans did. They have to propel cohesive clusters beyond their local interests and identities, and they must eliminate outsider thinking by creating superordinate challenges to focus on.

5. **Facilitate diversity into the core.** Diversity must be pulled into the core of the network to ensure greater agility, and peer reviews such as "Real, Win, Worth" should be utilized to engage people from varying backgrounds and experiences to scrutinize ideas for impact.

10

•────────────•

Close the Network

A social movement that only moves people
is merely a revolt. A movement that changes
both people and institutions is a revolution.

—MARTIN LUTHER KING JR.

In April 1963, Chandler Laughlin produced a unique musical experience at the Red Dog Saloon in the remote historic mining town of Virginia City, Nevada. The music was a mixture of traditional folk and an emerging psychedelic rock, featuring musical acts that were relatively unknown at the time, such as Jefferson Airplane, the Charlatans, and the Grateful Dead.[1] The experience was tribal-like, where people partook in peyote while freely expressing themselves through dancing and other antics during a psychedelic light show. They called this the "Red Dog Experience," and each night a small group would gather as a cohesive community to share in it. This experience was the emergence of an entrepreneurial pocket.

At the end of the summer of 1965, a few of the Red Dog Experience participants, acting as brokers, traveled back to San Francisco to establish their own community. They formed another group modeled on their experience in Virginia City with even the name remaining similar, The Family Dog. On October 16, 1965, they hosted San Francisco's first psychedelic rock performance featuring Jefferson Airplane, among other artists, and it served as the first of many such gatherings of hippies in San Francisco. The Family Dog hosted performances in such venues as the Avalon Ballroom and the Fillmore Auditorium. The vibe from the community spread quickly across the local region to experiences at the Longshoreman's Hall, Golden Gate Park, and Berkeley.

The proximity of these events enabled a movement, as the buzz of these experiences grew and echoed. Following this energy, bands like the Charlatans and Big Brother and the Holding Company, as well as the Grateful Dead, migrated into San Francisco's Haight-Ashbury neighborhood. Soon after, college and high-school students began flocking to Haight-Ashbury. Both the reputation and size of the growing subculture started attracting local media attention, so local officials did everything they could to halt the influx of young people. However, the conflict with officials unintentionally elevated the exposure in the national media, generating even more interest from young people. During mid-1967, a social phenomenon exploded with as many as 100,000 people herding into Haight-Ashbury for the Summer of Love.

Over the next few years, the movement spread across the United States as hippies cloaked themselves in floral fabrics and carried flowers while demonstrating for peace on the city streets. Advocating love over war, they marched in anti-war rallies in cities such as New York, Washington, D.C., and Chicago, and massed together in 1969 at the Woodstock Festival on a dairy farm in Bethel, New York. The event was later captured in the film *Woodstock: 3 Days of Peace and Music*. Over 400,000 people joined to hear the most notable musicians of the time, such stars as Janis Joplin, Santana, Jimi Hendrix, and the Grateful Dead. In total, 32 bands performed during the muddy weekend in what is widely proclaimed as a revolutionary moment in music history and the nexus for a counterculture movement. Indeed, while Woodstock was the pinnacle event for the hippie movement, the echo of this subculture shifted national beliefs with an insistence for freedom, authenticity, and community expression. As Martin Luther King Jr. once said, "A movement that changes both people and institutions is a revolution," and it all started with one small, cohesive pocket in Virginia City, Nevada.

It might seem strange to conclude a business book with a story about a psychedelic countercultural movement of hippies. However, in today's world of choosing either to positively disrupt or be disrupted, a countercultural perspective may be what is most needed. In today's dynamic environment, organizations need to be more liquid than static, and yet many organizations continue to operate with solidly outdated control and command models. They continue to fortify highly effective operational systems that drive alignment and efficiencies. Adaptive Space can enable this necessary shift by leaning into social rather than human capital strategies to increase the flow and velocity of idea diffusion, thereby creating positive disruption.

The social movement of hippies is a great analogy to demonstrate the dynamics necessary to operate in Adaptive Space. Small, cohesive entrepreneurial pockets, much like the Red Dog in Virginia City, need to be cultivated on the edges. Organizations need to provide the freedom for people to find a friend to experiment, the way a small group from Virginia City created The Family Dog. Organizations also need to set boundaries so that the energy from these small pockets, instead of dissipating, can echo from one to another, much as it did in San Francisco, as the vibe spread easily from the Fillmore Auditorium, to the Longshoreman's Hall, and then to Golden Gate Park. Organizations also need to consider how they enable this energy to attract others from across the network to engage in critical activities, the way young people followed the energy and flocked into the Haight-Ashbury neighborhood. Finally, organizations need to charge into the conflict to accelerate liftoff, just as the hippies gathered and tangled with the local officials, elevating exposure from the national media.

Adaptive Space is a countercultural perspective for enabling agility. This is what's called for when conventional wisdom breaks down. Remember the alpha male silverback gorilla. In response to external threats, these creatures instinctually organize their troop into a large huddle in order to look fiercer. This is conventional wisdom. However, this behavioral strategy just makes them an easier target when new intruders, namely poachers with guns, are the threat. In much the same way, in today's positively disrupt-or-be-disrupted world, the biggest threat to organizations isn't other large organizations. Today's business disruptors, or at least many of them, originated in another entrepreneurial pocket, just 40 miles south of San Francisco.

Setting Boundaries for Agility

In 1956, the coinventor of the transistor, William Shockley, started his own semiconductor company in Mountain View,

California. Shockley was a rock star in his profession, having been elected as a member of the National Academy of Sciences at only 41 years old, and being chosen as the recipient of the prestigious Comstock Prize for Physics. Even more impressive, he was a co-recipient of the Nobel Prize in physics as one of the inventors of the point-contact transistor. Based on his reputation, Shockley was able to attract some of the industries' best and brightest. However, some of these new colleagues quickly became disgruntled by Shockley's autocratic, erratic, and hard-to-please management style. Eight of these employees, or the "Traitorous Eight," as Shockley labeled them, ultimately decided to venture out on their own to start Fairchild Semiconductor.

Their start-up went on to become an enormously rich entrepreneurial pocket, developing some of the most important innovations of the twentieth century and spawning Silicon Valley.[2] The "Traitorous Eight" were the energizers of a new industry, spreading their passions and starting such companies as Intel, AMD, and the famous venture fund Kleiner Perkins, thereby setting the geographical boundaries for the semiconductor industry, which ultimately evolved into the world's high-tech haven. In fact, over the next two decades more than 65 start-ups were spawned from employees with connections to Fairchild.[3] Over the years, this number has grown to over 2,000 companies that can be linked to the "Traitorous Eight" entrepreneurial pocket.

The energy generated by Fairchild created an attraction for start-ups that was similar to the flocking of young people into the Haight-Ashbury neighborhood. Companies such as Atari, Apple, and Oracle were founded in the 1970s, soon followed by eBay, Yahoo, PayPal, and Google during the Internet era.

Today, Silicon Valley is widely recognized as the tech-centric hub for bold new start-ups. It can also be thought of as a vibrant ecosystem that nurtures the development of would-be disruptors. Each year CNBC issues its "Disruptor 50" list, featuring "innovative private companies in the world that are shaking up industries and causing major paradigm shifts that affect every corner of society."[4] The list represents progressive companies that have identified unexploited niches in the marketplace and have the potential to grow significantly and therefore disrupt existing corporate behemoths. Amazingly, more than half of the companies on this list reside in Silicon Valley.

In biology, an ecosystem is a community of living organisms interacting as a broader system. It is a group of interconnected elements operating within the same environment. For example, a coral reef is an ecosystem made up of diverse species that interact in symbiotic exchanges with each other while living within a defined physical environment. The structure of a reef is made up of microscopic invertebrates that spread out over coral skeletons and years of debris. This skeleton sets the boundaries of the reef ecosystem. It provides the edges that encourage the rich interaction of diverse creatures such as fish, anemones, sponges, shrimps, crabs, and other small animals. Some of these relationships are mutually beneficial, such as an anemone's tentacles providing a refuge for clownfish and their eggs, and the banded coral shrimp, which removes parasites from reef fish. Others are more combative, such as the coral crab, searching the reef for sea urchins and clams and crushing them with its powerful claws. Silicon Valley operates much in the same manner. Its distinct boundaries force a set of rich social interactions, with some providing support and refuge, while others prove to be combative. In either case, they serve to create the conflict necessary for a company to strive for faster liftoff.

The actual borders of Silicon Valley are often debated. It is geologically bounded by San Francisco Bay to the north and east, and the Santa Cruz Mountains to the west. These natural boundaries have created the edges for a rich set of social relationships like that of a coral reef. Additionally, numerous entrepreneurial pockets are surrounded by a kind of Adaptive Space that encourages social exchanges around such domains as silicon chip technology, computer design, and more recently, mobile apps. This space proves fertile for brokers to connect and then migrate from company to company in the pursuit of discovery, while connectors lock down, in cohesive clusters of start-ups, to fiercely develop the next big concept under a shroud of secrecy. Energizers play their role by buzzing up the ecosystem and diffusing ideas across the valley through networking platforms such as accelerators, incubators, and other informal exchanges. Finally, challengers provoke disruption by breaching conventional wisdom, charging into unexploited niches in the marketplace, and ushering in the new normal.

Just consider the ride hailing services of Uber and Lyft. They have had a disastrous effect on the taxi industry. By tapping into the sharing economy, these services offer less expensive and more convenient rides. On the other hand, the traditional taxicab empires and the cities they operate in have spent years building up fortified operational systems where they are effectively controlled much like a public utility. That is, the industry is heavily regulated with officials tightly controlling such things as the licensing of drivers and the fares that can be charged, and some cities, such as New York, Boston, and Chicago, use a "medallion system" where officials limit the number of cabs that can operate. Consequently, it is easy to see how ride hailing services have significantly disrupted this system. For example, the cost of a New York City taxi medallion, which at its peak would have fetched up to $1.3 million, has currently dropped to about one-fifth of this cost.[5] Perhaps even worse, cab drivers are now flocking to Uber and Lyft, forcing many taxicab companies across the United States to file for bankruptcy. The incubator for these disruptions has been the Adaptive Space of Silicon Valley.

This is the same mentality that needs to be applied within organizations as they charge into a positively disrupt or be disrupted type of landscape. Adaptive Space requires that organizations apply ecosystem thinking internally, enabling space for entrepreneurial pockets to emerge and connect for greater success. Organizations need to generate a small company mentality in the midst of a larger ecosystem, intentionally interacting in a resourceful manner, creating symbiotic exchanges and conflicting encounters, all while recognizing that each is beneficial to agility. They then need to set boundaries for these interactions to echo and diffuse without dissipation.

The Power of Proximity

Boundaries were critical to the GM2020 initiative. Launched in southeast Michigan as a grassroots movement to positively disrupt the way the company worked, it provided the Adaptive Space necessary to enable brokers to navigate across teams in an effort to discover innovations. It then tapped into the cohesive trust of connectors to encourage its local teams to implement these discoveries. Finally, the initiative unleashed buzz from energizers to spread these ideas from pocket to pocket throughout the organization. These dynamics could only happen because the initiative was ultimately bounded. That is, boundaries were set to limit focus on southeast Michigan to ensure these interactions could easily echo. Originally, the initiative focused on most of Michigan, but energy started to dissipate quickly after events. When the boundaries were tightened to include only four major sites, the echo immediately increased. Boundaries helped to facilitate interactions by creating greater proximity. Much like the San Francisco Bay and Santa Cruz Mountains bound the valley to create a concentrated set of high-tech interactions, physical closeness proved essential in generating contagious energy.

Furthermore, by reining in the number of sites, the GM2020 initiative increased liftoff. The formal activities such as Co-Labs, Summits, and the Tipping Forward celebration acted as catalyst events to provide a burst of energy for the local teams at the four sites, compelling each of these sites to create their own design teams to facilitate local activities. The energy also generated greater interest for individuals to be part of the core events, and the number of voluntary coaches supporting the summits quadrupled. More important, the overall community rapidly grew from just 60 people during the first event to thousands of community members walking around with GM2020 badges. Proximity clearly matters. This is one of the reasons we see organizations pulling people back into physical working spaces. Virtual working environments are fine when driving activities inside the operational system, but a dispersed network of employees will indeed limit the likelihood of positively contagious exchanges and therefore limit agility.

Nicholas Christakis and James Fowler's research taught us that energy ripples in a contagious manner across a network through our friends' friends' friends. There is another critical element to contagious energy, however. While our friends are close to us, they are not necessarily close to one another, and certainly not to our friends' friends. This is why boundaries become so critical. They create a container that enables echoes to bounce back into the community by connecting people further removed in the network. Remember the mass hysteria cases at LeRoy High School, the U.S. Navy barracks in San Diego, and the rural high school in North Carolina. They all had one thing in common: they were each tightly confined within a bounded community. In fact, 70 mass hysteria outbreaks were identified across two decades.[6] Fifty percent of those outbreaks took place in schools, and another 40 percent were confined to either small towns or factories. Only a mere 10 percent of these cases took place in broader settings. Indeed, it seems that an individual's emotions and energy are significantly more contagious in a tightly bounded network.

To further this understanding, let us again consider the coral reef example. A smaller, tighter reef creates the possibility for a richer set of exchanges within the ecosystem and forces cooperative, symbiotic behaviors and more combative exchanges, both of which serve in creating a more robust reef. This is what happened within the GM2020 community. Tighter boundaries encouraged more exchanges, which generated more peer-to-peer buzz, resulting in network closure on key decision makers. As more people were attracted to the initiative, leaders eventually became more interested. This enabled actions to more readily break through the leadership social bubble previously discussed. Indeed, the echo generated from the community helped to influence the leaders, and this phenomenon was then demonstrated as part of a network study that was conducted within the community. Members were asked to identify leaders who had sponsored or funded actions that were initiated by community members, and it was surprisingly determined that 95 percent of leaders had no formal connections to GM2020. Nevertheless, based on the bottom-up network buzz from their employees, the leaders were willing to sponsor changes. Echo helped to close the network and generate leadership support.

The hippie movement, Silicon Valley, and GM2020 all prove that proximity is fundamental to creating and maintaining momentum across a network. If individuals aren't talking about an idea, it can't gain momentum. Energy generates buzz across a network so that ideas and concepts can quickly spread. If the network is too broad, these same ideas can dissipate quickly. As a result, network boundaries need to be set so that the most critical brokers, connectors, and energizers are included. This also means that others need to be excluded. In general, ongoing proximity is critical to generating network buzz and creating an echo effect around creative solutions.

Network Closure Engages Leaders

While Facebook didn't exactly originate in Silicon Valley, it has certainly earned an honorary place there. We all know the story of how Mark Zuckerberg, as a sophomore, hacked into Harvard's student records and quickly threw together a basic website that paired classmates' photos. Facemash.com displayed student pictures side by side so viewers could decide who was "hot" and who was "not." He forwarded the link to several campus group list-servers and the use spread quickly, and within just four hours, the site had 450 visitors with 22,000 photo views.

When school officials were alerted, however, they shut down Zuckerberg's Internet connection. Many students were outraged with him, and the administration charged Zuckerberg with a breach of security, copyrights infringements, and violating individual privacy. He was forced to publicly apologize and shut the site down. All was not lost, however, as Zuckerberg had been inspired by the Facemash incident.

In February of 2004, he launched Facebook (then called The Facebook), profiling Harvard students, and by the end of the first month, over half of the undergraduate population had registered.[7] With his early success at Harvard, he then decided to extend to Columbia, Stanford, and Yale. Indeed, Zuckerberg knew that these schools already had campus-wide social networks, and he reasoned that if Facebook concentrated its efforts at Harvard and it caught on, the other schools would easily follow suit. Zuckerberg was right.

There is another story behind this story, however. Facebook very cleverly used an exclusivity deployment strategy, launching one cluster at a time. That is, a friend would invite you to join, and you could only register if you went to one of the current universities. In other words, if a friend from Columbia sent you an invite, but you were an NYU student, you would have to wait until your school's site had been launched before you could join. This strategy proved brilliant in rocketing up the demand for the site, but what Zuckerberg failed to anticipate was how socially contagious this strategy would be. Each school was a concentrated social cluster with clearly defined boundaries that were even tighter than the boundaries of San Francisco's hippie movement or Silicon Valley's technological uprising. The social clusters of each school made it fairly easy to tip registrations for each one. Furthermore, when you added in the exclusivity model as an amplifier, it only took a matter of hours for a new school to register most of its students. Initially each school was its own island, but over time Facebook began to connect schools, creating even greater buzz. The strategy worked well, and by November of 2004, Facebook had registered its one-millionth user. Only three months later, the site had two million active users and had been deployed at 370 schools. This is exponential growth by any measure.

Facebook tapped into the power of cohesion by building a social network one cluster at a time. It closed the broader network by connecting the clusters. It also tapped into the proximity effect by leveraging the propensity of behaviors and ideas to spread more quickly within a cohesive cluster. Organizations can do the same thing internally. Rather than pitching their ideas upward into the hierarchy, employees can tap into the power of clusters or entrepreneurial pockets to create buzz. They can then seed the broader network by opening up connections for people, ideas, information, and resources to come together. Organizations can create Adaptive Space so their people can freely explore, exchange, and debate in order to be positively disruptive.

In December of 2012, Doug Burger, a Microsoft researcher in system architecture, was asked to present his thinking during an internal technology review. The group included the company's then-CEO, Steve Ballmer, along with many of his top lieutenants in Building 99, the company's big bet research lab just outside Seattle. At this review, Burger presented his belief that the tech world was about to move into a new orbit, and he argued that Internet services would become so complex that companies would have to build a whole new architecture to run them.[8] He said that Google and Amazon were already taking steps in this direction, and he went on to suggest that the world's hardware providers wouldn't deliver what Microsoft needed for its online services. Unfortunately, Ballmer didn't buy his argument.

This certainly wasn't because of Burger's credentials. Burger isn't an ordinary technology guy. He is one of the world's leading researchers in computer architecture, with an extensive list of contributions. Only four years before joining Microsoft, he had been a full professor at the University of Texas at Austin, where he co-led a project that remains one of the most complex microprocessor prototypes ever built in academia. His research also contributed to the non-uniform cache architectures, which continue to operate within Intel, ARM, and IBM microprocessors.

Of course, none of this mattered to Ballmer. He ran a software company, and to his way of thinking, a researcher was arguing why the company needed to develop hardware. The boisterous CEO had been expecting an update on research, not a strategy briefing, and accordingly, he continued to grill Burger. At some point another voice joined in the conversation, however, and it was one of Ballmer's key lieutenants, Qi Lu. Lu ran Microsoft's search engine, Bing, and his team had been working with Burger and other researchers on reprogrammable computer chips for nearly two years. The name of the project was Catapult. Lu had personally experienced the power of this work, and he was therefore able to vouch for Burger's expertise. Lu was able to "close the network" in on Ballmer, or, you could say, he catapulted Burger's reputation inside the social bubble.

Remember, people from outside the bubble have two major challenges before them. First, they need a compelling case for their idea, and then they must convince the insiders that they are worth listening to. Lu was an insider who provided Burger with instant credibility. Most of us would like to believe that our reputations emerge based on the merit of our work and our positive behaviors. We want to cite competence as king. The truth, however, is that our reputations materialize not as much from what we actually do as from people talking about what we do. Sociologist Ron Burt describes this phenomenon as "gossip and reputation."[9] He has found that our reputation emerges from the stories exchanged about us within our network: in other words, from the gossip about us. His research suggests that accuracy is actually more of a nicety than a requirement, and what the network shares depends as much on the interests of people sharing the stories as it does on the stories they are sharing. Indeed, it is more about empathy than competence. If someone isn't interested in a story we are sharing, we intuitively shift the way we are sharing it, even if we inadvertently distort the actual story to do so. Therefore, gossip is much less about the person being talked about and much more about the people doing the talking. Other people's interests form our reputations. Gossip is how this information echoes. Inside a cohesive network, the gossip or echo is what quickly forges a reputation.

This is the real brilliance of Doug Burger. He joined Microsoft because he was compelled to do something boldly innovative from a hardware perspective. He knew he couldn't do this alone, so he found a friend in software expert Jim Larus and partnered with him. Together, in recognizing that selling a hardware solution within a software company would be incredibly difficult, they started to think about where there might be a Trojan horse. Indeed, they knew that the company wouldn't make a huge investment in the technology without a direct application. So the duo spent nine months meeting with the Bing team, trying to understand what they might be able to do with custom hardware. They knew that Google was the titan of search and already had the dominant position of mindshare, with excessive volumes of data and huge reserves of money to continue to invest. Burger, however, thought that silicon scaling was about ready to reach the law of diminishing returns, and he therefore hypothesized that architecture would have to change significantly.[10] After evaluating opportunities within Bing, the duo focused on developing an advantage with the ranking algorithms, reasoning that if they could make them significantly faster, they could improve accuracy.

It was at this point that they partnered with Andy Putnam, an expert in FPGAs, which are programmable chips that are more agile than the general-purpose CPU, or central processing unit. FPGAs, or field programmable gate arrays, are customizable so they can handle the new problems in an ever-shifting operating environment. Putnam built a prototype that could run Bing's machine-learning algorithms about 100 times faster than the traditional CPU. The Bing team was certainly interested by this time, but they didn't like the prototype. Bing engineers argued that a solution with only six FPGAs and a rack full of servers was a problem. Furthermore, the complexity of machine learning would likely need even more computing power than six FPGAs. So they started working on a second prototype. This one included a giant pool of connected programmable chips that any Bing machine could leverage. It was a major improvement over the first prototype, and the network of Bing engineers started to positively gossip about it. The Trojan horse was both interesting and relevant to Bing, and ultimately Qi Lu endorsed it, providing Burger and the team the funding to build and test over 1,600 servers equipped with FPGAs.

Two years later, when Burger was presenting to Ballmer and his lieutenants, he wasn't just another technology guy; he had forged the social capital and reputation necessary to break through the bubble. As an insider, Qi Lu was willing to vouch for Burger. Today the company uses FPGA technology well beyond Bing. Microsoft Azure uses these programmable chips to route data, and Office 365 is migrating toward FPGAs for encryption and compression capabilities. Lu helped to close the network for Burger, and together, within the network, they positively disrupted Microsoft.

Interestingly enough, sociologists suggest that when we announce ourselves or try to substantiate our own credibility, we are generally discounted. However, if someone else does it on our behalf, our credibility is amplified. For example, Stanford researcher Jeffrey Pfeffer and colleagues conducted a study in which an audience was asked to rate the favorability of writers based on two identical excerpts touting the author's accomplishments.[11] In the first scenario, the authors read the excerpts about themselves. In the second scenario, which the audience always rated as more favorable, a representative read the excerpt on behalf of the author. This is why it is so critical to get our network talking about us. People naturally listen more favorably to another person touting our accomplishments than to us tooting our own horns. To forge a positive reputation, much in the same manner as Burger's Trojan horse example, however, they need to be talking about something that is relevant or at least interesting to them and others.

Reputation spreads through gossip and echoes across a given cluster. Over time, this can close the network on a given concept, increasing the likelihood of others being invited into the inner circle to share the idea, building both sponsorship and formal endorsement. This is essential to generating support and positioning ideas for support from the operational system. This dynamic is very different from blindly pitching an idea to leaders. By tapping into the gossip and reputation process, the network does much of the work, and as individuals across the network engage in the advancement of an idea, others are attracted to engage, and the network begins to close in around a sponsor. Eventually an insider like Qi Lu takes notice, closing the network in on other leaders.

Adaptive Space Principles in Practice

In January of 2015, GM held a Co-Lab designed to create a way for employees to communicate innovative ideas in response to given vehicle challenges. The focus was to use a Co-Lab to create the Adaptive Space necessary for employees to share, exchange, and critique ideas on an open and continuing basis, whereby multiple prototypes were generated and evaluated by a panel of executive judges. It was the find-a-friend strategy after the event, however, that proved to be the most instrumental to the organization. For example, one participant, Ehaab, went and found a friend, Ahmad Hares, a young engineer. Ehaab knew that this was a topic that Hares would be interested in. Over the next year, the duo grew into a team of volunteers that went on to develop a set of innovation solutions that far surpassed any of the prototypes from the first event.

This passionate band of innovators created Lightbox, a speaking series in which GM and industry leaders share ideas; they launched a crowdsourcing solution called Tackle; and finally, they launched a new innovation challenge process. It is this last creation that best exemplifies the various principles of Adaptive Space. The innovation challenge process began with engaging the edges. Hares was at an external event when he experienced a rapid cycle innovation process that included a series of *Shark Tank*–like pitches. He thought to himself, "Could this connect GM employee ideas to our customers?" From there, he went and found Ehaab, and together they mapped out a process that included three progressive pitches that would fast-track innovative concepts competitively. At the conclusion of this process, the goal was to have one or two concepts fully funded and supported to proceed in the vehicle development process. They called this process Synapse, representing the new pathways created to get innovations into the system.

Hares and Ehaab were able to secure support rather rapidly by following the energy and taking on a challenge that needed additional support, filling in a void on an existing vehicle technology road map. They began this process with another Co-Lab that used design thinking methods to collect insights from customers. Over the course of two days, 75 cross-functional employees volunteered to work in small, diverse teams that actively engaged customers in empathy interviews focusing on how they used their vehicles, with some even riding shotgun with the customers to learn customer driving patterns and other behaviors on nearby streets.

At the end of the two days, these teams pitched their prototypes to a leadership team to gain endorsement. This meant that an executive would agree to personally support, coach, and fund the next stage of advancement for a given team. Nine teams were selected to proceed to the next stage.

For the next six weeks these teams were given access to cost engineering, marketing, and design support, and they were called to charge into the conflict of the real-world realities to advance their ideas. Finally, the nine competed in another executive review, and this time the thresholds for selection were even more intense, with only four of the nine teams proceeding to the final round. After getting some tough feedback to enhance their efforts, these four competed in a final face-off in front of nearly 700 employees, and in the end, two major concepts were formally endorsed for development. Today, Synapse provides employees the opportunity to plunge into design thinking with critical innovation challenges. As many as 30 teams and up to 200 colleagues have the chance to step into the customers' shoes to understand how they feel about such things as ride sharing. They then sketch out concepts, build prototypes, and battle it out with each other.

The development of Synapse embodies the Adaptive Space principles. Both engaged the edges: Ehaab by inviting customers into the Co-Lab, while Hares drew on his external shark tank experience. They quickly came together as friends and then followed the energy by testing and iterating on multiple concepts. Conflict was built into the process through feasibility reviews. They were first able to close the network in on a core group of leaders, who then closed the network more broadly by connecting 700 additional employees. This all began with two junior engineers, Ehaab and Hares, who opened up Adaptive Space designed to positively disrupt the innovation process within GM.

Conclusion

In a positively disrupt or be disrupted world, agility is more vital than ever. Organizations must swiftly morph and adapt, like Netflix. They need to create discovery connections to identify unexploited market opportunities and then quickly develop these concepts so they can be brought to life. Organizations must also tap into the power of networks to rapidly diffuse these ideas. Finally, they need to be willing to positively disrupt themselves in the never-ending quest toward new possibilities, just as Netflix disrupted the DVD-by-mail business to move toward online streaming, and then migrated to original content. Like Lewis and Clark, they must map out new territories that spur curiosity from others and compel them to travel forward. To do so, they need to open up Adaptive Space so people can freely explore, exchange, and debate ideas.

Adaptive Space is the secret of agile organizations. It is why organizations such as Facebook, IBM, Gore, and Amazon are adaptive. These organizations know that social interactions are crucial. They know that agility isn't exclusively the result of human capital; network position matters. They are passionate about social capital and how well someone is positioned to leverage what he or she knows. These organizations leverage the power of brokers to discover, tap into the development capabilities of connectors, position energizers to openly diffuse ideas, and finally, usher in a new normal through the disruptive connections of challengers. Adaptive Space facilitates the interconnectivity of people, ideas, information, and resources. It provides the relational freedom for people to openly explore and exchange ideas. It also provides the emotional freedom necessary for debate and disruption. Adaptive Space is the antecedent to agility. It helps to overcome the stifling effects of the operational system on critical entrepreneurial activities.

General Motors, in its recent efforts, has aggressively enabled Adaptive Space to position itself for the inevitable disruption of the oncoming mobility revolution, while at the same time delivering daily results. The company has quietly gone from bankruptcy to producing record profits in one of the most successful business turnarounds in the modern age. GM is leaner, more agile. The question is simple, however: Can GM operate with the velocity necessary to positively disrupt itself? Or will a more agile organization get there first?

In today's dynamic environment, the adage "adapt or die" has become the new reality, and Adaptive Space has become the path forward.

Acknowledgments

This book would not have been possible without the support of an incredible research team led by Mary Uhl-Bien from Texas Christian University. I am especially indebted to Rob Cross, Professor of Global Leadership at Babson College. His two decades of research on organizational networks and his personal mentorship to me is foundational to this book. I am also grateful to Alex "Sandy" Pentland, who introduced me to the power of social capital and networks while at the MIT Media Lab. I truly appreciate the insights and guidance from both Glenn Carroll, Professor of Organizational Behavior from Stanford Business School, and Wayne Baker, Professor of Management and Organizations from Ross School of Business at the University of Michigan.

I am also grateful to all of those whom I have had the pleasure to work with during this process. Greg Pryor, Chris Ernst, and Nat Bulkley were instrumental in sharing network insights. Laurie Asava, Rachel Rosenbaum, Karie Mielke, and Kelly Kuras were critical collaborators on the GM2020 journey. Perry Klebahn, Jeremy Utley, and Kathryn Segovia from the Stanford d.school provided ongoing inspiration. Prucia Buscell helped me in the editing, proofreading, and design.

Finally, this book would not have been possible without the learning journey of the "odd fellows," Sharon Benjamin, Bill Kirkwood, Cary LeBlanc, and Alan Barstow. Nobody has been more important to me in this pursuit than the members of my family. I would like to thank my parents, for their love and guidance. My three wonderful children, Alyssa, Amanda, and Anthony, who encouraged me in spite of all the time I spent away from them. Most important, I want to thank my wife, Lisa, for her incredible advice, countless edits, and ongoing encouragement. It was a long and difficult journey.

Research Summary

Recognizing that research and practice had been mute on the question of how to position people and organizations for agility, a research team set out to understand the dynamics necessary for enabling organizational adaptability. The team could see that change was coming. Pressures emanating from a more dynamic operating environment were growing, and they weren't going to go away. The team could also see that our current understanding and approaches weren't meeting the need. They were developed for a previous era when the problems facing organizations were about managing physical assets for efficiency and control. In this framework, leaders are being trained in hierarchical models that aren't working as well in today's faster, more demanding, informal work environments. The things they are practicing are actually making things worse.

The research team was co-led by Mary Uhl-Bien from the Neeley School of Business at TCU and myself. The team also included Russ Marion, Craig Schreiber, and Ivana Milosevic. The primary research question for the study was, *"What is the process by which ideas emerge and flow in the organization?"* Focus was placed on the dynamics that contributed to idea generation, how ideas flowed into and across the organization, and what factors influence these processes.

The challenge was immense and would require a multifaceted approach. It could not be accomplished with a single research study or through the work of academics or practitioners alone. It required a partnership between academic research and practice that would develop both a rigorous, evidence-based body of findings and a relevant, experience-based understanding of how leading for agility actually works. Therefore, we began with Russ and Mary's review of the academic literature and development of a theoretical model for understanding agility in a complex world. We then delved deeply into practice to see the extent to which the theoretical predictions held true, and where adjustments were needed to increase the validity and reliability of the model. A practice team was created that included Dana Baugh, an executive coach and organizational development consultant and previously a global lead at the Gallup Organization; Brad Anderson, retired CEO of Best Buy; Debra France, an executive in enterprise leadership development and learning design at W.L. Gore and Associates; Sharon Benjamin, a leading expert in adaptive positive deviance at Plexus Institute; and Anne Harbison, an expert in adaptability who studied with Ron Heifetz and Robert Kegan at Harvard.

By the time we were through we had conducted nearly 400 interviews in organizations across a range of industries, from aerospace, healthcare, and high-tech firms to financial services, consumer goods, and automotive. We coded and analyzed these interviews to evaluate the findings in the context of our theoretical framework. Throughout this process, researchers and practitioners engaged intensively in interpreting the findings through both a research lens and a practice lens. We also gathered quantitative data through network analysis and energy and engagement surveys to help us understand the internal organizational dynamics associated with innovation and agility in organizations. This became even more important as we began to realize the role and importance of networks to Adaptive Space.

The culmination of the research-practice partnership occurred when I took the position at GM in 2012. I began engaging principles from our theoretical framework into my practice work to help unleash talent at GM in ways that could enable agility and adaptation for the organization. I then had regular phone calls and check-ins with Mary to see how the process was going, with Mary interviewing me at various stages of my efforts to gather evidence on how the model was working and where we needed to make further refinements. This led to invaluable understanding of the challenges and intricacies associated with leading for organizational agility. With this rich, deeply nuanced theoretical and practical understanding, we confirmed our model and conducted a final validation against highly innovative and adaptive organizations.

Notes

CHAPTER 1

1. "Cisco's John Chambers on the Digital Era," McKinsey & Company High Tech, Interview, March 2016, https://www.mckinsey.com/industries/high-tech/our-insights/ciscos-john-chambers-on-the-digital-era.
2. Ashley Rodriguez, "Netflix Was Founded 20 Years Ago Today Because Reed Hastings Was Late Returning a Video," Quartz, August 29, 2017, https://qz.com/1062888/netflix-was-founded-20-years-ago-today-because-reed-hastings-was-late-a-returning-video/.
3. Michelle Castillo, "Reed Hastings' Story About the Founding of Netflix Has Changed Several Times," CNBC, May 23, 2017, https://www.cnbc.com/2017/05/23/netflix-ceo-reed-hastings-on-how-the-company-was-born.html.
4. Rita Marini, "Keeping the Customer Romance Alive Protects Your Business from Extinction," *Digitalist Magazine*, August 3, 2017, http://www.digitalistmag.com/customer-experience/2017/08/03/keeping-customer-romance-alive-protects-business-from-extinction-05248355.
5. Ilan Mochari, "Why Half of the S&P 500 Companies Will Be Replaced in the Next Decade," *Inc.*, March 23, 2016, https://www.inc.com/ilan-mochari/innosight-sp-500-new-companies.html.

6. Ray Oldenburg, *The Great Good Place: Cafés, Coffee Shops, Community Centers, Beauty Parlors, General Stores, Bars, Hangouts, and How They Get You Through the Day* (New York: Paragon House, 1989).

7. Greg Satell, "A Look Back at Why Blockbuster Really Failed and Why It Didn't Have To," *Forbes*, September 5, 2014, https://www.forbes.com/sites/gregsatell/2014/09/05 /a-look-back-at-why-blockbuster-really-failed-and-why-it -didnt-have-to/#e7fe4a51d64a.

8. Stephen Edelstein, "GM May Partner with Uber on Self-Driving Cars, Report Says," The Drive, October 20, 2017, http://www.thedrive.com/sheetmetal/15316/gm-may -partner-with-uber-on-self-driving-cars-report-says.

9. "Why GM Wants Out of Europe After Nearly 90 Years: Quick Take Q&A," Interview by Chad Thomas, Bloomberg, February 14, 2017, https://www.bloomberg .com/news/articles/2017-02-14/why-gm-wants-to-sell -opel-after-nearly-90-years-quicktake-q-a.

10. Melissa Burden, "Global Retreat Shrinks GM Footprint," *Detroit News*, May 18, 2017, http://www.detroitnews.com /story/business/autos/general-motors/2017/05/18/gm-stop -sales-india-exit-africa-market/101822544/.

CHAPTER 2

1. Lawrence Levy, "How Steve Jobs Became a Billionaire," *Fortune*, October 19, 2016, http://fortune.com/steve-jobs -pixar-apple-lawrence-levy/.

2. Ibid.

3. Jeff Kays, "This Day in Pixar History: Pixar IPO," November 29, 2012, http://www.thisdayinpixar.com/2012/11/this -day-in-pixar-history-pixar-ipo.html.

4. Ronald S. Burt, *Brokerage and Closure: An Introduction to Social Capital* (Oxford, New York: Oxford University Press, 2005).

5. Robert L. Mitchell, "How MasterCard Restructured for IT Innovation," *Computerworld*, February 25, 2013, https://www.computerworld.com/article/2474222/it-leadership/how-mastercard-restructured-for-it-innovation.html.

6. André Vermeij, "How Steve Jobs Connected It All: An Interactive Look at Apple's Technology History," Kenedict, December 11, 2014, https://www.kenedict.com/how-steve-jobs-connected-it-all-an-interactive-look-at-apples-technology-history/.

7. Linus Dahlander and Siobhan O'Mahony, "A Study Shows How to Find New Ideas Inside and Outside the Company," *Harvard Business Review*, July, 2017, https://hbr.org/2017/07/a-study-shows-how-to-find-new-ideas-inside-and-outside-the-company.

8. Stefan Wuchty, Benjamin F. Jones, and Brian Uzzi, "The Increasing Dominance of Teams in Production of Knowledge," *Science* 316, no. 5827 (2007): 1036–1039.

9. "'Mosh Pits of Creativity: Innovation Labs are Sparking Teamwork—and Breakthrough Products," Bloomberg, November 6, 2005, https://www.bloomberg.com/news/articles/2005-11-06/mosh-pits-of-creativity.

10. Richard Behar, "Inside Israel's Secret Startup Machine," *Forbes*, May 11, 2016, https://www.forbes.com/sites/richardbehar/2016/05/11/inside-israels-secret-startup-machine/#60e3545e1a51.

11. "GM to Test Autonomous Cars on Israel's Roads," *Globes*, June 15, 2017, http://www.globes.co.il/en/article-gm-to-test-autonomous-cars-on-israels-roads-1001192727.

12. "Based on Chevrolet's Bolt Electric Car, the Prototype Is Being Tested on Public Highways in Israel," *Globes*, June 14, 2017, http://www.globes.co.il/en/article-gm-israel-unveils -autonomous-car-prototype-1001192500.

CHAPTER 3

1. Mary Bellis, "Thomas Edison's Muckers," updated April 5, 2017, https://www.thoughtco.com/thomas-edisons-muckers -4071190.
2. "Inventing Edison's Lamp," http://americanhistory.si.edu /lighting/19thcent/invent19.htm.
3. Lee Fleming, Santiago Mingo, and David Chen, "Collaborative Brokerage, Generative Creativity, and Creative Success," *Administrative Science Quarterly* 52, no. 3 (2007): 443–475.
4. Lee Fleming, "Finding the Organizational Sources of Technological Breakthroughs: The Story of Hewlett-Packard's Thermal Ink-jet," *Industrial and Corporate Change* 11, no. 5, November 1, 2002, 1059–1084.
5. Rob Cross, Reb Rebele, and Adam Grant, "Collaborative Overload," *Harvard Business Review*, January–February 2016.
6. Mark Buchanan, "The Science of Subtle Signals," *Strategy+Business* 48, August 29, 2007.
7. Jasjit Singh and Lee Fleming, "Lone Inventors as Sources of Breakthroughs: Myth or Reality?," *Management Science* 56 (1), 41–56.
8. André Vermeij, "Apple's Internal Innovation Network Unraveled – Part 2 – Apple's Industrial Design Team," Kenedict, March 9, 2013, https://www.kenedict.com/apples -internal-innovation-network-unraveled-part-2-apples -industrial-design-team/.

9. Janet Choi, "The Science Behind Why Jeff Bezos's Two-Pizza Team Rule Works," *I Done This* (blog), September 24, 2014, http://blog.idonethis.com/two-pizza-team/.

10. John Brandon, "Meet the Founder Trying to Start the Self-Driving Car Revolution," *Inc.* magazine, February 2015, https://www.inc.com/magazine/201502/john-brandon/the-new-cruise-control-kyle-vogt-cruise-automation.html.

11. Erin Griffith, "Driven in the Valley: The Startup Founders Fueling GM's Future," *Fortune*, September 22, 2016, http://fortune.com/cruise-automation-general-motors-driverless-cars/.

12. Ibid.

13. Ibid.

14. "Start Spreading the News: GM's Self-Driving Cars Head to New York," *Fast Company*, October 17, 2017, https://www.fastcompany.com/40482593/start-spreading-the-news-gms-self-driving-cars-head-to-new-york.

15. Emily Chang and Anne Riley Moffa, "GM Clutches Tech Units Despite Hype of $30 Billion Spinoff," *Automotive News*, October 17, 2017, http://www.autonews.com/article/20171017/OEM/171019690/&template=print.

16. "GM Produces First Round of Self-Driving Chevrolet Bolt EV Test Vehicles," GM Media, June 16, 2017, http://media.gm.com/media/cn/en/gm/news.detail.html/content/Pages/news/cn/en/2017/June/0613_GM-Produces-First-Round-of-Self-Driving.html.

17. Colonel Ardant Du Picq, *Battle Studies: Ancient and Modern Battle*, 1921, https://www.gutenberg.org/files/7294/7294-h/7294-h.htm.

18. Michael J. Arena, Alex (Sandy) Pentland, and David Price, "Honest Signals; Hard Measures of Social & Human

Behavior," *Organizational Development Journal* 28 (3) (2009): 11–20.

CHAPTER 4

1. Eric Markowitz, "From Start-up to Billion-Dollar Company," *Inc.*, April 6, 2012, https://www.inc.com/eric -markowitz/alibaba-film-dawn-of-the-chinese-internet -revolution.html.

2. Calum MacLeod, "Alibaba's Jack Ma: From 'Crazy' to China's Richest Man," *USA Today*, September 17, 2014, https://www.usatoday.com/story/tech/2014/09/17/alibaba -jack-ma-profile/15406641/.

3. Rob Cross, Wayne Baker, and Andrew Parker, "What Creates Energy in Organizations?," *MIT Sloan Management Review* 44 (2003): 51–57.

4. "Southwest Flight Attendant Comforts Girl When She Panics on Flight," AJC.com, July 20, 2016, http://www.ajc.com /news/national/southwest-flight-attendant-comforts-girl -when-she-panics-flight/Z2Qx4ba7n3lI5wOiaV7BAJ/.

5. Shawn Tully, "Southwest Bets Big on Business Travelers," *Fortune*, September 23, 2015, http://fortune.com/2015/09 /23/southwest-airlines-business-travel/.

6. Alex Pentland and Tracy Heibeck, *Honest Signals: How They Shape Our World* (Cambridge, MA: MIT Press, 2010).

7. GM Press Release, "Mary Barra Outlines GM's Road Map for Safer, Better and More Sustainable Transportation Solutions," September 15, 2017, http://media.gm.com /media/cn/en/gm/news.detail.html/content/Pages/news /cn/en/2017/September/0915_Mary-Barra-Outlines-GM -Road-Map.html.

8. Ibid.

9. Nicholas Christakis and James Fowler, *Connected: The Surprising Power of Our Social Networks and How They Shape Our Lives* (New York: Little Brown, 2009).

10. Rick Tetzeli, "GM to Top Tech Talent: Ditch Silicon Valley for Detroit," *Fast Company*, October 17, 2016, https:// www.fastcompany.com/3064642/gm-to-top-tech-talent -ditch-silicon-valley-for-detroit.

CHAPTER 5

1. Drew Guarini, "Relentless.com Is a Secret Way You Can Get to Amazon.com," *Huffington Post*, October 15, 2013, https://www.huffingtonpost.com/2013/10/15/amazon -relentless-secret-site_n_4100916.html.

2. Hal Gregersen, "The One Skill That Made Amazon's CEO Wildly Successful," *Fortune*, September 17, 2015, http://fortune.com/2015/09/17/amazon-founder-ceo-jeff -bezos-skills/.

3. Brian Smale, "Bezos on Innovation," *Bloomberg*, April 17, 2008, https://www.bloomberg.com/news/articles/2008-04 -16/bezos-on-innovation.

4. David Kirkpatrick, "Wired and Shrewd, Young Egyptians Guide Revolt," *New York Times*, February 9, 2011, http://www .nytimes.com/2011/02/10/world/middleeast/10youth.html.

5. Mary Bellis, "The IBM 701: The History of International Business Machines and IBM Computers," updated April 5, 2017, https://www.thoughtco.com/the-ibm-701 -1991406.

6. Steven Musil, "William Lowe, the 'Father of the IBM PC,' Dies at 72," CNET, October 28, 2013, https://www.cnet .com/news/william-lowe-the-father-of-the-ibm-pc-dies-at -72/.

7. Ted C. Fishman, "What Happened to Motorola," *Chicago* magazine, August 25, 2014, http://www.chicagomag.com /Chicago-Magazine/September-2014/What-Happened-to -Motorola/.

8. Sharon Reier and International Herald Tribune, "Half a Century Later, Economist's 'Creative Destruction' Theory Is Apt for the Internet Age: Schumpeter: The Prophet of Bust and Boom," *New York Times*, June 10, 2000, http://www .nytimes.com/2000/06/10/your-money/half-a-century -later-economists-creative-destruction-theory-is.html.

9. Joseph Schumpeter, *Capitalism, Socialism and Democracy* (New York: Harper, 1975 [orig. pub. 1942]), 82–85.

10. Sharon Reier and International Herald Tribune, "Half a Century Later, Economist's 'Creative Destruction' Theory Is Apt for the Internet Age." *New York Times*, June 10, 2000, http://www.nytimes.com/2000/06/10/your-money /half-a-century-later-economists-creative-destruction -theory-is.html.

11. Charles A. O'Reilly and Michael Tushman, "Ambidexterity as a Dynamic Capability: Resolving the Innovator's Dilemma," *Research in Organizational Behavior* 28 (2008): 185–206.

12. Nick Bunkley, "Mark Reuss, in the 'Knothole,'" *Automotive News*, May 22, 2017, http://www.autonews.com /article/20170522/OEM02/305229997/mark-reuss-in-the -knothole.

13. Greg Gardner, "GM's Bolt EV Team, Up Against Short Deadline, Delivers," *Detroit Free Press*, March 12, 2016, https://www.freep.com/story/money/cars/general-motors /2016/03/12/gms-bolt-ev-team-up-against-short-deadline -delivers/81448772/.

14. Robert Sutton, "The Weird Rules of Creativity," *Harvard Business Review* (September 2001): 94–103.
15. Michael Hogg, "A Social Identity Theory of Leadership," *Personality and Social Psychology Review* 5, no. 3 (2001), 184–200.
16. Margaret Heffernan, "Willful Blindness: When a Leader Turns a Blind Eye," *Ivey Business Journal*, May/June 2012.
17. Claudia Deutsch, "At Kodak, Some Old Things Are New Again," *New York Times*, May 2, 2008, http://www.nytimes.com/2008/05/02/technology/02kodak.html?mtrref=www.google.com&gwh=31812F34823EFD8C4C93C34BD2428359&gwt=pay.

CHAPTER 6

1. Ronald Burt, "Structural Holes and Good Ideas," *American Journal of Sociology* 110 (2004): 349–399.
2. Larry Huston and Nabil Sakkab, "Connect and Develop: Inside Procter & Gamble's New Model for Innovation," *Harvard Business Review*, March 2006.
3. Elizabeth Gudrais, "Innovation at the Intersection," *Harvard Magazine*, May–June 2010, https://harvardmagazine.com/2010/05/innovation-at-the-intersection.
4. Jonny Fisher, "What Does Facebook Stories Say About Facebook's Innovation Output?," April 6, 2017, http://ideadrop.co/facebook-stories-innovation/.
5. Farhad Manjoo, "Why Facebook Keeps Beating Every Rival: It's the Network, of Course," *New York Times*, April 19, 2017.
6. Nikolaus Franke and Sonali K. Shah, "How Communities Support Innovative Activities," *Research Policy* 32, no. 1 (2003): 157–178.

7. Eric von Hippel and Mary Sonnack, "Breakthroughs to Order at 3M," Working Paper, January 1999, http://web.mit.edu/evhippel/www-old/papers/3M%20Breakthrough%20Art.pdf.

8. Elana Zak, "How Twitter's Hashtag Came to Be," *Wall Street Journal*, October 3, 2013, https://blogs.wsj.com/digits/2013/10/03/how-twitters-hashtag-came-to-be/.

9. Robert Campbell, "The State of Stata," *Boston Globe*, March 11, 2007.

10. Sharon Benjamin, Prucia Buscell, Denise Easton, Laura Gardner, and Irene McHenry, *Unexpected Gifts: Solve Tough Problems with Adaptive Positive Deviance* (Washington, D.C.: Plexus Institute, 2017), 12.

11. Gina Shaw, "A Deviant Approach to Hospital Challenges," November 2009, https://acphospitalist.org/archives/2009/11/positive.htm.

12. Brad Powers, "How Coca-Cola Uses Entrepreneurs (and Keurig) to Jump-Start Innovation," Forbes Leadership Forum, October 8, 2015, https://www.forbes.com/sites/forbesleadershipforum/2015/10/08/how-coca-cola-uses-entrepreneurs-and-keurig-to-jump-start-innovation/#59a7c6be481e.

13. Benjamin et al., *Unexpected Gifts*, 12.

CHAPTER 7

1. Neil Tambe, "W. L. Gore: A Case Study in Work Environment Redesign," Deloitte Insights, June 19, 2013, https://www2.deloitte.com/insights/us/en/topics/talent/w-l-gore.html.

2. Derick Sivers, "How to Start a Movement," TED2010, https://www.ted.com/talks/derek_sivers_how_to_start_a_movement.

3. Alan Deutschman, "The Fabric of Creativity," *Fast Company*, December 1, 2004.
4. James Surowiecki, *The Wisdom of Crowds* (New York: Anchor Books, 2005).
5. Chris Weller, "Apple Made a Simple Design Choice in 2001 That Sent It into the Stratosphere," *Business Insider*, June 1, 2016, http://www.businessinsider.com/why-are-apple-headphones-white-2016-5.
6. Gene Weingarten, "Pearls Before Breakfast: Can One of the Nation's Great Musicians Cut Through the Fog of a D.C. Rush Hour? Let's Find Out," *Washington Post*, April 8, 2007.
7. Pádraig MacCarron, Kimmo Kaski, and Robin Dunbar, "Calling Dunbar's Numbers," *Social Networks* 47 (2016): 151–155.
8. Solomon E. Asch, *Social Psychology* (Englewood Cliffs, NJ: Prentice Hall, 1952).
9. Mithu Storoni, "The Extraordinary Reason Exceptional People Avoid Mediocre Friends (They Rewire Your Brain)," *Inc.*, June 28, 2017, https://www.inc.com/mithu-storoni/the-extraordinary-reason-exceptional-people-avoid-mediocre-friends-they-rewire-y.html.
10. Joshua Porter, "The Freedom of Fast Iterations: How Netflix Designs a Winning Web Site," UIE, November 14, 2006, https://articles.uie.com/fast_iterations/.
11. Rob Cross, Chris Fussel, Alia Crocker, and Peter Gray, "Organizational Agility: How Targeted Network Investments Promote Organizational Responsiveness," White Paper, Connected Commons, September 2017.
12. James Heskett, *The Culture Cycle: How to Shape the Unseen Force That Transforms Performance* (Upper Saddle River, NJ: FT Press, 2012), 126–127.

13. Daniel Ariely, *Predictably Irrational: The Hidden Forces That Shape Our Decisions* (New York, NY: HarperCollins, 2008).

14. Teresa M. Amabile, Sigal G. Barsade, Jennifer S. Mueller, and Barry M. Staw, "Affect and Creativity at Work," *Administrative Science Quarterly* 50, no. 3 (September 2005): 367–403.

CHAPTER 8

1. Ryan Jaslow, "Mass Hysteria Outbreak Reported in N.Y. Town: What Does It Mean?," *CBS News*, January 19, 2012, https://www.cbsnews.com/news/mass-hysteria-outbreak -reported-in-ny-town-what-does-it-mean/.

2. "U.S. Experts Blame Anxiety for Illness of West Bank Girls," Special to the *New York Times*, April 26, 1983, http://www.nytimes.com/1983/04/26/world/us-experts -blame-anxiety-for-illness-of-west-bank-girls.html.

3. Joseph Menn, "117 of Ill Recruits Returned to Base," September 5, 1988, *LA Times*, http://articles.latimes.com/1988 -09-05/local/me-1019_1_navy-recruits.

4. Susan Dominus, "What Happened to the Girls in Le Roy," *New York Times*, March 7, 2012, http:// www.nytimes.com/2012/03/11/magazine/teenage-girls -twitching-le-roy.html?mcubz=0&mtrref=undefined.

5. Nicholas Christakis and James Fowler, *Connected: The Surprising Power of Our Social Networks and How They Shape Our Lives* (New York: Little, Brown, 2009).

6. Sarah Fister Gale, "It Takes a Village," *Chief Learning Officer*, September 30, 2016, http://www.clomedia.com/2016 /09/30/34728/.

7. Chuck Blakeman, "DaVita: A 65,000 Person Corporate Village, or Just a CEO's Nutty Dream?," *Inc.*, November 11,

2015, https://www.inc.com/chuck-blakeman/davita-a-65
-000-person-corporate-village-or-just-the-ceo-s-nutty
-dream.html.

8. Jane E. Dutton, *Energize Your Workplace: How to Create and Sustain High-Quality Connections at Work* (San Francisco, CA: Jossey-Bass, 2003).

9. Sigal Barsade, "Faster than a Speeding Text: 'Emotional Contagion' at Work," *Psychology Today*, October 15, 2014, https://www.psychologytoday.com/blog/the-science-work /201410/faster-speeding-text-emotional-contagion-work.

10. Larry Hardesty, "A Social Network That Ballooned," *MIT News*, December 11, 2009, http://news.mit.edu/2009/red -balloon-challenge-1211.

11. "Case Study: Bank of America," *Bloomberg*, June 19, 2006, https://www.bloomberg.com/news/articles/2006-06-18 /case-study-bank-of-america.

12. Guy Boulton, "By Turning Medical Scans into Adventures, GE Eases Children's Fears," *Journal Sentinel*, January 21, 2016, http://archive.jsonline.com/business/by-turning -medical-scans-into-adventures-ge-eases-childrens-fears -b99647870z1-366161191.html/.

13. "Slack's Founder on How They Became a $1 Billion Company in Two Years," *Fast Company*, February 4, 2015, https://www.fastcompany.com/3041905/slacks-founder-on -how-they-became-a-1-billion-company-in-two-years.

14. Bryony Reich, "The Diffusion of Innovations in Social Networks," Working Paper, 2016.

15. "How Design Thinking Transformed Airbnb from a Failing Startup to a Billion Dollar Business," *The Review*, http:// firstround.com/review/How-design-thinking-transformed -Airbnb-from-failing-startup-to-billion-dollar-business/.

CHAPTER 9

1. Frank Nugent, "Snow White and the Seven Dwarfs," Review, *New York Times*, January 14, 1938.

2. Charles Solomon, "Movie Review: 'Snow White,' 50, Still Sets Standards," *LA Times*, July 16, 1987, http://articles.latimes.com/1987-07-16/entertainment/ca-4233_1_snow-white.

3. "Walt Disney Acted Out Snow White and All Its Characters on Stage to Inspire His Team to Make the Movie," *TheJournal.ie*, September 27, 2015, http://www.thejournal.ie/walt-disney-documentary-2343806-Sep2015/.

4. Clayton Christensen, "Innovation: A Happy Meal for McDonald's," *Forbes*, October 26, 2007, https://www.forbes.com/2007/08/31/christensen-innovation-mcdonalds-pf-guru_in_cc_0904christensen_inl.html#7a3de2157422.

5. Linda A. Johnson, Associated Press, "Against Odds, Lipitor Became World's Top Seller," *USA Today*, updated December 28, 2011, https://usatoday30.usatoday.com/news/health/medical/health/medical/treatments/story/2011-12-28/Against-odds-Lipitor-became-worlds-top-seller/52250720/1#mainstory.

6. Donelson R. Forsyth, *Group Dynamics*, 5th ed. (United States of America: Wadsworth Cengage Learning, 2009).

7. Margaret Heffernan, "Dare to Disagree," TEDGlobal 2012, https://www.ted.com/talks/margaret_heffernan_dare_to_disagree.

8. Carmel McCoubrey, "Alice Stewart, 95; Linked X-Rays to Diseases," *NY Times*, July 4, 2002, http://www.nytimes.com/2002/07/04/world/alice-stewart-95-linked-x-rays-to-diseases.html.

9. "Leading Creativity: Lessons from Pixar," Recharted Territory, December 11, 2015, https://www.rechartedterritory.com/leading-creativity-lessons-pixar/.

10. David Segal, "An Oasis in a Desert of Customer Service," *New York Times*, June 8, 2013, http://www.nytimes.com/2013/06/09/your-money/at-quicken-loans-a-culture-geared-to-customer-service.html?mtrref=www.google.com.

11. "ISMs," Quicken Loans Press Room, https://www.quickenloans.com/press-room/fast-facts/#isms.

12. Amanda Lewan, "Quicken Loans Innovates with a 'Small Business' Culture," *Michipreneur*, March 5, 2013, http://www.michipreneur.com/quicken-loans-innovates-with-a-small-business-culture/.

13. Maria Konnikova, "Revisiting Robbers Cave: The Easy Spontaneity of Intergroup Conflict," *Scientific American*, September 5, 2012, https://blogs.scientificamerican.com/literally-psyched/revisiting-the-robbers-cave-the-easy-spontaneity-of-intergroup-conflict/.

14. "What Really Happens at Mixers?," Ideas at Work, Columbia Business School, February 27, 2007, https://www8.gsb.columbia.edu/articles/ideas-work/what-really-happens-mixers.

15. Vivian Hunt, Dennis Layton, and Sara Prince, "Why Diversity Matters," McKinsey, January 2015, https://www.mckinsey.com/business-functions/organization/our-insights/why-diversity-matters.

16. Ann Harrington, "Who's Afraid of a New Product? Not W.L. Gore," *Fortune* magazine, November 10, 2003, http://archive.fortune.com/magazines/fortune/fortune_archive/2003/11/10/352851/index.htm.

CHAPTER 10

1. "Sex, Drugs and Rock n' Roll," http://sexdrugs-rocknroll.blogspot.com/2007/05/19601966.html.

2. Rhett Morris, "The First Trillion-Dollar Startup," *Tech Crunch*, July 26, 2014, https://techcrunch.com/2014/07/26/the-first-trillion-dollar-startup/.

3. Rhett Morris and Mariana Penido, "How Silicon Valley Became 'Silicon Valley,' " Report, Endeavor Insight, July 2014, https://issuu.com/endeavorglobal1/docs/hdsvbsv__final_.

4. "Meet the 2016 CNBC Disruptor 50 companies," CNBC, updated May 16, 2017, https://www.cnbc.com/2016/06/07/2016-cnbcs-disruptor-50.html.

5. Tim Stenovec, "More Proof That Uber Is Killing the Taxi Industry," *Business Insider*, January 7, 2016, http://www.businessinsider.com/more-proof-that-uber-is-killing-the-taxi-industry-2016-1.

6. Margaret Talbot, "Hysteria Hysteria," *New York Times Magazine*, June 2, 2002, http://www.nytimes.com/2002/06/02/magazine/hysteria-hysteria.html.

7. Sarah Phillips, "A Brief History of Facebook," *The Guardian*, July 25, 2007, https://www.theguardian.com/technology/2007/jul/25/media.newmedia.

8. Cade Metz, "Microsoft Bets Its Future on a Reprogrammable Computer Chip," *Wired*, September 25, 2016, https://www.wired.com/2016/09/microsoft-bets-future-chip-reprogram-fly/.

9. Ron Burt, "Gossip and Reputation," in *Management et Réseaux Sociaux: Ressource Pour l'Action ou Outil de Gestion?*, ed. Marc Lecoutre and Pascal Lievre (London: Hermes-Lavoisier, 2008), 27–42.

10. Allison Linn, "The Moonshot That Succeeded: How Bing and Azure Are Using an AI Supercomputer in the Cloud," Microsoft Blog, October 17, 2016, https://blogs .microsoft.com/ai/the_moonshot_that_succeeded/.
11. Jeffrey Pfeffer, Christina T. Fong, and Robert B. Cialdini, "Overcoming the Self-Promotion Dilemma: Interpersonal Attraction and Extra Help as a Consequence of Who Sings One's Praises," *Personality and Social Psychology Bulletin* 32, no. 10 (November 2006), 362–374, http://journals.sagepub .com/doi/abs/10.1177/0146167206290337.

Index

Page numbers followed by *f* refer to figures.

About the Author

Michael J. Arena, PhD, is an acclaimed speaker and author of the groundbreaking research on Adaptive Space that won the 2017 Walker Prize from People + Strategy. He is a leading expert in organizational network analysis, and his work has been cited in the *Wall Street Journal*, *Harvard Business Review*, *Business Insider*, *Sloan Management Review*, and *Chief Executive* magazine. Arena is also the Chief Talent Officer for General Motors (GM) and has played a critical role in the company's transformation. He launched GM2020, a grassroots initiative designed to enable employees to positively disrupt the way they work, which was highlighted in *Fast Company*. Arena also teaches in Penn's Masters in Organizational Dynamics program and acts as a design thinking coach within the Stanford d.school. Prior to joining GM, he spent two years as a visiting scientist within MIT's Media Lab where he studied networks and served as a Senior Vice President of Leadership Development at Bank of America.